U0100537

大展好書　好書大展

品嘗好書　冠群可期

大展好書　好書大展

品嘗好書　冠群可期

中英文對照武學(5)

李壽堂 編著　　張連友 校訂

42式 太極劍 學與練

附VCD

大展出版社有限公司

42式太極劍學與練

Study and Practice of 42-form Tai Chi Sword

作者　李壽堂

Writer　Shoutang Li

翻譯者　北美意源書社
　　　　孫慧敏　姜淑霞

Translator　Huimin Sun, Yiyuan Martial Arts Books, North America
　　　　　　Shuxia Jiang, Yiyuan Martial Arts Books, North America

作者李壽堂和張連友的練功照

孫國慶演示的42式太極劍

前 言

42式太極劍套路分四段42個動作，演練時間爲3至4分鐘。其中包括十八種不同劍法，五種不同步型，三種不同組別的平衡，三種腿法和三個不同的發勁動作。

這套太極劍是國家體委武術研究院於20世紀90年代初組織國內武術名家以「繼承、發展、創新」爲目的，以「傳統性、科學性、健身性、競賽性」爲原則進行創編的。42式太極劍既保留了傳統太極劍的風格特點，又有所創新；不僅内容充實，動作規範，結構嚴謹，編排新穎，布局合理，而且動作數量、組別和時間等都符合競賽規則的要求，目前已成爲國内外武術比賽的項目之一。

Preface

42–form Tai Chi Sword is divided into 4 groups, including 42 movements, taking 3 to 4 minutes to complete. There are 18 sword strokes, 5 step forms, 3 stances, 3 leg movements and 3 force–launching actions involved in this form. Supported by the Wushu Institution of the Chinese Sports Committee, this set of Tai Chi Sword was created at the beginning of 90s in 20th century by famous Wushu experts for the purpose of inheriting, developing and innovating traditional Wushu culture. It follows the principle of inheriting tradition, complying with science, benefiting health and also suitable for competition. The 42– form Tai Chi Sword has retained the styles and features of traditional Tai Chi sword as well as gained new characteristics. It has rich content, standardized action, sound structure, original arrangement and rational layout. The number of movements, groups and the time it takes are all compliant with the requirements of competitions. Thus, it now has become an event in both national and international Wushu games.

目　錄

Content

42式太極劍的基本動作規格

Basic Techniques of 42-form Tai Chi Sword

一、手型和手法

手 型

太極劍的手型就是指劍指。即中指、食指併攏伸直，其餘三指屈於手心，大拇指壓在無名指及小指第一指節上。

手 法

手法是指握劍的方法。

1. Hand Forms and Hand Movements

Hand Forms

The main hand form is the Sword Fingers (Jian zhi). To form Sword Fingers, extend the index finger and the middle finger together and bend the other two fingers to the palm with the thumb pressing on their first knuckle.

Hand Movements

Hand Movement in Tai Chi Sword means the ways of holding a sword.

1. 持 劍

手心貼緊護手，食指附於劍柄，拇指和其餘手指扣緊護手，劍脊輕貼前臂後側。

(1) Carrying

The palm presses around the hand guard of the sword

tightly with the index finger resting on the handle, the thumb and other three fingers supporting sides of the hand guard. The sword spine makes slight contact with the backside of the arm.

2. 握劍

正握劍——立劍（刃向上下），小指側刃在下。

反握劍——立劍，小指側刃在上。

俯握劍——平劍（刃向左右），手心向下。

仰握劍——平劍，手心向上。

(2) Gripping

Forhand Gripping (Zheng Wo Jian)

Grip a sword with one edge up and one edge down. The edge at the same side with the fingers is facing down.

Backhand Gripping (Fan Wo Jian)

Grip a sword with one edge up and one edge down. The edge at the same side with the fingers is facing up.

Palm Down Gripping (Fu Wo Jian)

Grip a sword with the blade flat. Palm is facing down.

Palm Up Gripping (Yang Wo Jian)

Grip a sword with the blade flat. Palm is facing up.

【要領】

（1）手腕要鬆，手指要活，手心要空。

（2）握劍以拇指、中指和無名指為主，食指、小指配合，隨動作靈活掌握，時鬆時緊，順其自然。

Key Points

(1) When gripping the sword, keep the wrist relaxed, the fingers flexible and the palm empty (a bit away from the handle).

(2) The force of the grip comes mainly from the thumb, the middle finger and the third finger, with the index finger and little finger co-operating. Connect the motions naturally; do not be rigid.

二、步型和步法

1. 步 型

（1）弓 步

前腿全腳著地，腳尖向前，屈膝不得超過腳尖，最好與湧泉穴上下相對；後腿自然伸直，避免僵直硬挺，腳尖斜向前約45°，全腳著地，兩腳橫向距離10～20公分。

2. Foot Positions and Foot Movements

(1) Foot Positions

a. Bow Step (Gong Bu)

Place the entire front foot on the ground, the toes pointing forward. Bend the knee without over the toes; it is about perpendicular to the toes. The other leg stretch naturally straight, but avoid being stiff. And the toes point at about 45° inwards with foot planted on the ground. The feet are on parallel lines, which distance is about 10 to 20 cm.

(2)馬 步

兩腳左右開立，約腳長的三倍；腳尖正對前方，外撇不超過30°，屈膝半蹲。膝與腳尖同方向。

b. Horse Step (Ma Bu)

The feet stand apart with the distance between them about three times of the foot length (about 60cm). The toes point for-ward or outward less than 30° . Bend knees in a half squat and in the same directions with the toes.

(3)虛 步

一腿屈膝半蹲，全腳著地，腳尖斜向前45°；另一腿微屈，以前腳掌或腳跟點地於身前，兩腳之間距離不小於一腳。

c. Empty Step (Xu Bu)

Bend one knee with the entire foot placed on the ground and toes outward 45° . Bend the other knee slightly with either only the forefoot or only the heel of the foot on the ground. The distance between the feet should not be less than a foot (about 20 cm).

(4)仆 步

一腿屈膝全蹲，膝與腳尖稍外展；另一腿自然伸直，平鋪接近地面，腳尖內扣，兩腳全腳著地，不可掀起。

d. Crouch Stance or Step (Pu Bu)

One leg bends in a squat, the knee and toes pointing slightly outwards. Extend the other leg close to the ground, toes pointing inward. Both feet are fully placed on the ground.

(5)丁 步

一腿屈膝半蹲，全腳著地；另一腿屈膝，以腳前掌或腳尖點於支撐腿腳內側。兩腳距離小於一腳。

e. T－shape Step (Ding Bu)

Bend one leg in a half squat with the foot placed on the ground. Bend the other knee with its forefoot or toes touching the ground at the inside of the supporting foot. The distance between the feet should not be over a foot.

(6)歇 步

兩腿屈膝全蹲，前腳尖外展，全腳著地；後腳尖向前，膝部附於前腿外側，腳跟離地，臀部接近腳跟。

f. Low Squat with Crossed legs (Xie Bu)

Bend the two legs in a squat. The front toes turns outward

with the sole fully touching the ground. The knee behind attaches to the inside of the front knee with the toes pointing forward and the heel is lifted off the ground. The buttocks should be close to the heel as if sitting on it.

(7)獨立步

一腿自然直立，支撐站穩；另一腿在體前或體側屈膝提起，高於腰部，小腿自然下垂，腳面展平，腳尖不可上蹺。

g. One Leg Stand or Independent Step (Du Li Bu)

One leg stands straight naturally, supporting the weight. The other one lifted with the knee bent in front or at side of the body at waist level, and the lower leg droops down naturally. The foot should be stretched and the toes pointing downward naturally.

(8)平行步

兩腳分開，腳尖向前，屈膝下蹲，兩腳外緣與肩同寬。

h. Parallel Step (Ping Xing Bu)

Place the feet apart at the shoulder width, toes pointing forward and knees bent in a half squat.

2. 步 法

（1）上步。後腳經支撐腿內側向前上一步或前腳向前半步。

（2）活步。前（後）腳隨動作稍做移動。

（3）退步。前腳經支撐腿內側後退一步。

（4）撤步。前（後）腳退半步。

（5）蓋步。一腳經支撐腳前橫落。

（6）插步。一腳經支撐腳後橫落。

（7）跳步。前腳蹬地跳起，後腳前擺落地。兩腳同時有一瞬間的騰空。

（8）行步。腿微屈，兩腳連續上步，步幅均勻，重心平穩，不得起伏。

（9）擺步。上步腳落地時腳尖外擺，與後腳成八字步。

（10）扣步。上步腳落地時腳尖內扣，與後腳成八字步。

（11）跟步。後腳向前跟進半步。

（12）碾步。以腳跟為軸，腳尖外展或內扣，或以腳前掌為軸，腳跟外展。

各種步法進退轉換要做到輕靈穩健，虛實分明。前進時，腳跟先著地；後退時，前腳掌先著地，萬萬不可滯重突然。重心移動要平穩、均勻、充分、清楚。兩腳距離和跨度要適當。腳掌腳跟輾轉要適度，膝部自然鬆活，直腿時不可僵直。

(2) Foot Movements

a. Forward Step (Shang Bu)

The back foot takes a step forward, past the inside of the supporting foot or the front foot takes a half step forward.

b. Moving Step (Huo Bu)

Keep the front or the back foot moving during the movement.

c. Backward Step (Tui Bu)

The front foot takes a step backward, past the inside of the supporting foot.

d. Withdraw Step (Che Bu)

The front (or back) foot takes a half step backward.

e. Crossover Step (Gai Bu)

One foot steps forward crossing over the supporting foot.

f. Crossover Backward Step (Cha Bu)

One foot steps back crossing over the supporting foot.

g. Jump Step (Tiao Bu)

The front foot jumps up and the back foot swings forward and lands on the ground.

h. Walking Step (Xing Bu)

The legs bend slightly and the feet move forward alternately with even steps. Meanwhile shift the weight steadily without up and down.

i. Toes Out Step (Bai Bu)

Step forward with one foot. When the foot is placed on the ground, turn the toes outward to form a "\ /" shape with the back foot.

j. Toes In Step (Kou Bu)

Step forward with one foot. When the foot is placed on the ground, turn the toes inward to form a "/ \" shape with the back foot.

k. Follow Up Step (Gen Bu)

The back foot follows the front foot by half a step.

l. Pivoting Step (Nian Bu)

Pivoting on the heel, turn the toes either inward or outward depending on the movement. Or, pivot on the forefoot and turn the heel outward or inward.

Various steps should be flexible and steady with distinction between emptiness and solidness. When stepping forward, the heel touches the ground first; When stepping backward, the forefoot touches the ground first. The movements should never be sluggish or abrupt. Shift the weight stably, evenly, completely and distinctly. The span between the feet should be appropriate and the pivoting movement of the heels or palm should be comfortable and smooth. The knee should be kept naturally relaxed;

do not be rigid when stretching the legs.

三、身型與身法

1. 身 型

（1）頭。向上虛虛領起，下頜微微內收，不可偏歪和搖擺。

（2）頸。自然豎直，肌肉不可緊張。

（3）肩。保持鬆沉，不可聳肩，不可後張前扣。

（4）肘。自然下墜，不可僵直、外翻、揚起。

（5）胸。舒鬆自然，不要外挺、內縮。

（6）背。自然放鬆，舒展拔伸，不可弓背。

（7）腰。自然放鬆，不後弓、前挺，運轉靈活，以腰為軸，帶動手足。

（8）脊。保持正直，不可左右歪斜、前挺後弓。

（9）臀、胯。臀要收斂，不可凸臀；胯要鬆、縮、正，不可左右歪扭。

（10）膝。伸屈柔和自然。

3. Body Form and Body Technique

(1) Body Form

a. Head

Upright; do not lean or swing. The chin is tucked in slightly.

b. Neck

Naturally upright and muscle relaxed.

c. Shoulders

Maintained relaxed and sunken. Do not lift them up or push forward or stretch backward.

d. Elbows

Sunken naturally. Do not be rigid or turned outward.

e. Chest

Naturally relaxed. Avoid straightened or tucked.

f. Back

Naturally relaxed, upright and stretched. Do not stoop.

g. Waist

Naturally relaxed. Do not be bent. Used as the axle of the body and limbs.

h. Spine

Maintained upright naturally. Do not lean in any direction.

i. Hips

Pulled in. Maintained upright. The hips should be relaxed, sunken, tucked in, and upright.

j. Knees

Extended or bent gently and naturally.

2. 身 法

身法上要求端正自然，不偏不倚，舒展大方，旋轉靈活。忌僵滯、浮軟，忽起忽落。以腰為軸，帶動上下，完整貫穿。

(2) Body Technique

The whole body is naturally upright, stretched, flexible, and comfortable. Avoid being rigid or too soft. Use the waist as the axle to lead the limbs and unify the whole body' s motions.

四、腿　法

1. 蹬 腳

支撐腿微微屈膝站穩；另一腿屈膝提起，勾腳，以腳跟為力點慢慢蹬出，腿自然伸直，腳高過腰。

4. Leg Technique

(1) Kicking with the Heel

The supporting leg stands steadily and bends slightly. Bend the other knee and lift the foot, toes pointing backward and kick out with force at the heel. Straighten the leg naturally, higher than the waist.

2. 分 腳

支撐腿微屈；另一腿屈膝提起，然後小腿上擺，自然伸直，腳面展平，不低於腰。

（2）Separating feet

Bend the supporting leg slightly. Bend the other leg and lift it, swing the lower leg upward and stretch it naturally, the foot stretched and higher than the waist.

3. 擺 腿

支撐腿微屈站穩；另一腿從異側擺起，經胸前向外擺動，擺幅不小於135°，腳面展平，不低於肩。

（3）Swing the foot

Bend the supporting leg slightly and stand steadily. Swing the other leg outward more than 135° from the other side of the body, the foot stretched and higher than the shoulder.

4. 震 腳

支撐腿微屈；另一腿提起，以全腳掌向地面踏震，勁須鬆沉。

（4）Stamping Step

Bend the supporting leg slightly. Lift the other foot and stamp it on the ground forcefully with the whole sole touching the ground. The force should be relaxed and heavy.

5. 後舉腿

支撐腿微屈站穩；另一腿在身後向異側方向屈

舉，腳面自然展平，腳掌心向上；上體稍傾斜，並向舉腿方向擰腰。

以上五種腿法均要支撐穩定，膝關節不可僵硬；上身中正，不可前俯後仰，左右歪斜。

(5) Lifting the foot Backward

Bend the supporting leg slightly and stand steadily. Bend the other leg backward and lift it towards the other side behind the body, the foot stretched and sole facing up. Lean the upper body slightly forward and twist the waist in the same direction with the leg lifted.

Five leg techniques mentioned above all need steady supporting. The knee should not be stiff. Keep the upper body upright without bending forward or backward and leaning left or right.

五、眼　法

定勢時，眼要看前方或劍、劍指；轉換時，要勢動神隨，神態自然。

5. Eye Technique

As each movement is finished, look ahead or at the sword or at the sword fingers. When connecting movements, eyes follow the hands or the sword with a natural expression.

六、劍　法

劍由劍身、劍格、劍柄、劍首等部分組成。

劍身又分為劍尖、劍鋒、劍刃、劍脊（圖1–1）。

劍的長度，以直臂垂肘反手持劍的姿勢為準，劍尖不得低於本人耳上端。劍可帶劍穗，劍的重量及劍穗長短不限。

6. Sword Technique

A sword consists of a blade, a guard, a handle and a pommel.

A sword blade includes a tip, a ridge, double edges and a spine (Figure 1–1).

The standard for the sword size: let the arm hang down and hold the sword pointing up. The tip of the sword should not be lower than the upper edge of the ear.

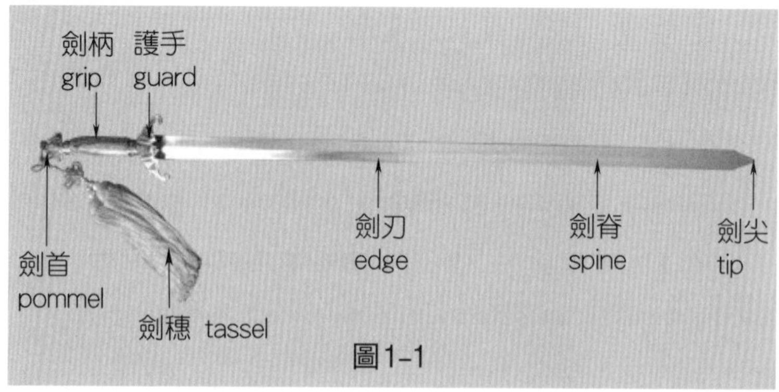

圖1–1

A sword can be decorated with a tassel. There is no demand for the weight and size.

1. 點 劍

立劍，提腕，使劍尖由上向前下點擊，臂自然伸直，力達劍尖下鋒。

(1) Pointing Down (Dian Jian)

Hold the sword, edge up. Raise the wrist, and let the tip of the sword point down. Stretch the arm naturally and deliver the force to the lower edge.

2. 削 劍

平劍，自異側下方經胸前向同側上方斜出為削。手心斜向上，劍尖略高於頭。

(2) Peel (Xiao Jian)

Hold the sword, blade flat. Wield the sword upward diagonally from the other side of the body to the side of the hand holding the sword, across the chest. The palm is facing diagonally up and the tip of the sword is slightly above the head.

3. 劈 劍

立劍，自上而下為劈，力達劍身。掄劈則須將劍掄一立圓，然後向前下劈。劈劍分上劈、中劈、下劈。

(3) Chop (Pi Jian)

Hold the sword, edge up. Chop down with the force on the blade. The Swing Chop (Lun Pi) is to swing the sword in a vertical circle with the shoulder acting as an axle, and cleave it down in front of the body. There are also Upper Chop (Shang Pi), Middle Chop (Zhong Pi) and Downward Chop (Xia Pi).

4. 攔 劍

攔劍分左攔劍和右攔劍。立劍，臂內旋，由左下向右前方斜出，腕高不過頭，低不過胸，劍尖向左前下，勁貫劍前刃為右攔劍。左攔劍與右攔劍動作相反，要領一致。

(4) Parry (Lan Jian)

There is a Left Parry and a Right Parry. Right Parry: Hold the sword with the edge up, turn the arm inward, and move the sword from the lower left to the front right until the wrist is at the level of the head. The tip of the sword points down to the lower front, force going through the front edge of the sword. The Left Parry is the same in the opposite direction.

5. 撩 劍

立劍，由下向前上方為撩，力達劍身前部為正撩劍，前臂外旋，手心朝上，貼身弧形撩出；反撩劍前臂內旋，其餘同正撩劍。

(5) Upward Slice (Liao Jian)

Hold the sword with its edge up. Wield the sword up in an arc with force going to the front part of the blade. Slicing Straight Up: turn the forearm outward until the palm faces upward, slicing up close to the body in an arc. Slicing Up, Towards the Back: turn the forearm inward until the palm faces outward, slicing up close to the body in an arc.

6. 刺 劍

立劍或平劍，向前直出為刺。勁達劍尖，臂與劍成一線，劍尖與胸平為平刺；劍尖略高於頭為上刺；劍尖與膝平為下刺。臂內旋，手心向外，劍經肩上側向前下（上）方立劍刺出為探刺。

(6) Thrust (Ci Jian)

Hold the sword with the blade flat or edge up and thrust it forward with force delivered to the tip, the arm and the sword in one line. When the tip is at chest level, it is called a Level Thrust; when the tip is at head level, it is called an Up Thrust (Shang Ci); the tip at knee level is called a Down Thrust (Xia Ci). Lean and Thrust (Tan Ci): turn the arm inward, palm facing outward; thrust the sword to the lower or upper front, along and above the shoulders.

7. 斬 劍

平劍，向右橫出，高在頭與肩之間，勁達劍身。

(7) Slash (Zhan Jian)

Hold the sword, blade flat. Slash horizontally to the right (or the left) at a height between the head and the shoulder. Deliver the force to the blade of the sword.

8. 崩 劍

立劍，沉腕，使劍尖向上，發力於腕，力達劍上鋒。

(8) Burst (Beng Jian)

Hold the sword, edge up. Sink the wrist and tilt the tip of the sword up. Deliver the force from the wrist to the upper edge.

9. 絞 劍

平劍，手心向上，以腕關節為軸，使劍尖由右向左逆時針小立圓繞環，力達劍身前部。

(9) Stirring (Jiao Jian)

Hold the sword, blade flat. The hand faces up and draws counter-clockwise ovals with the tip of the sword, the wrist acting as an axle. The force is on the front part of the blade.

10. 截 劍

劍身斜向上或斜向下為截，勁達劍身前部。上截劍斜向上；下截劍斜向下。

(10) Intercepting (Jie Jian)

Move the sword to the lower left or the lower right, with force going to the front part of the blade. Up Intercept is to move the sword diagonally up; Down Intercept is to move the sword diagonally down.

11. 帶 劍

平劍，由前向左或右屈臂回抽為帶，腕高不過胸，劍尖斜向前，勁貫劍身中後部。

(11) Withdraw (Dai Jian)

Hold the sword, blade flat. Draw the sword back from the front to the left (or right) by bending the arm. The wrist is lower than the chest and the tip points diagonally forward. Deliver the force to the lower part of the sword.

12. 托 劍

立劍，劍身平置，由下向上為托。手心向裏，腕與頭平，勁貫劍身中部。

(12) Holding Up and Lifting (Tuo Jian)

Hold the sword horizontally with edge up. Lift the sword

upward to head level with the palm facing inward. The force is on the middle part of the sword.

13. 穿 劍

立劍，劍貼身向下弧形運動，勁達劍尖。

(13) Stab (Chuan Jian)

Hold the sword with the edge up. Move the sword downward in an arc. The force reaches the tip of the sword.

14. 架 劍

立劍，手心向外，由下向右上方為架，劍高過頭，劍身橫直，勁貫劍身。

(14) Holding Up (Jia Jian)

Hold the sword horizontally with the edge up. Raise the sword to the upper right above the head, the palm facing outward. The force goes through the blade of the sword.

15. 掃 劍

平劍（劍為水平狀），向左或右平擺，擺幅大於90°，劍高不過腰，勁貫劍刃。

(15) Sweep (Sao Jian)

Hold the sword, blade flat. Sweep it to the left or the right over 90°, the highest point is lower than the waist. The force is concentrated on the edge of the sword.

16. 抹 劍

平劍，劍從一側經體前弧形向另一側抽帶為抹，高與胸平，劍尖向異側前方，勁達劍身。

(16) Slide (Mo Jian)

Hold the sword with the blade flat. Wield the sword in an arc from one side of the body to the other and across the front. The blade is at the level of the chest, the tip of the sword pointing the opposite direction. Deliver the force to the blade.

17. 雲 劍

平劍，在頭前方或上方平圓繞環為雲。

(17) Cloud (Yun Jian)

Hold the sword with the blade flat and draw big horizontal ellipses overhead or in front of the head.

18. 推 劍

劍身豎直，劍尖向上，手心向前，由後向左前或左推出，力達劍身中部。

(18) Push (Tui Jian)

Hold the sword, edge up. With the tip of the sword pointing up and the palm facing forward, push the sword towards the front left or the left. The force is on the middle part of the blade.

19. 掛劍

立劍，劍尖由前向下向同側或異側貼身掛出，勁貫劍身前部。

(19) Stab Back (Gua Jian)

Hold the sword, edge up. The tip of the sword goes back from either side of the body. The force is on the front part of the blade.

20. 壓劍

平劍，手心向下，向下壓劍，劍尖向前。

(20) Press (Ya Jian)

Hold the sword with the blade flat and press it down. The palm faces down and the tip of the sword points forward.

21. 提劍

立劍，手心向外，腕部上提同頭高或稍高於頭，劍尖斜向下。

(21) Raise (Ti Jian)

Hold the sword, edge up. Raise the wrist to be level with or slightly higher than the head. The palm is facing outward and the tip of the sword pointing down.

各種劍法要做到：劍法清楚，勁力順達，力點準確，身劍協調，方法正確。

One should clearly understand all the sword techniques. Deliver the energy smoothly and accurately. The sword and one's body always coordinate with each other. Practice the techniques with the correct methods.

42式太極劍動作名稱

42-form Tai Chi Sword Movements

預備式

第一組

1. 起　式　2. 併步點劍　3. 弓步削劍
4. 提膝劈劍　5. 左弓步攔　6. 左虛步撩
7. 右弓步撩　8. 提膝捧劍　9. 蹬腳前刺
10. 跳步平刺　11. 轉身下刺

第二組

12. 弓步平斬　13. 弓步崩劍　14. 歇步壓劍
15. 進步絞劍　16. 提膝上刺　17. 虛步下截
18. 右左平帶　19. 弓步劈劍　20. 丁步托劍
21. 分腳後點

第三組

22. 仆步穿劍（右）　23. 蹬腳架劍（左）
24. 提膝點劍（左）　25. 仆步橫掃（左）
26. 弓步下截（右、左）　27. 弓步下刺
28. 右左雲抹　29. 右弓步劈
30. 後舉腿架劍　31. 丁步點劍
32. 馬步推劍

第四組

33. 獨立上托	34. 進步掛劍	35. 歇步崩劍
36. 弓步反刺	37. 轉身下刺	38. 提膝提劍
39. 進步穿劍	40. 擺腿架劍	41. 弓步直刺
42. 收　式		

太極劍風格特點

意領劍隨	劍身合一	圈化圈發	避實擊虛
以腰帶劍	勁透劍身	手空劍活	劍法靈活
端莊典雅	柔中寓剛	輕靈沉穩	劍勢纏綿

Preparation

Group1

1. Opening
2. Point Sword Down and Feet Together
3. Peel in Bow Step
4. Chop and Lift the Knee
5. Parry in Left Bow Step
6. Upward Slice in Left Empty Step
7. Upward Slice in Right Bow Step
8. Hold Sword with Both Hands and Lift the Knee
9. Thrust Forward and Kick with the Heel

10. Jump and Thrust Flat
11. Turn Body and Thrust Down

Group 2

12. Horizontal Slash in Bow Step
13. Burst in Bow Step
14. Pressing Sword in Low Squat with Crossing Legs
15. Stirring and Marching
16. Thrust Upward and Raise Knee
17. Intercept Downward in Empty Step
18. Withdraw Sword – Right and Left
19. Chop in Bow Step
20. Lift Sword in T – Step
21. Separate Foot and Point Sword Back

Group 3

22. Thrust Sword in Crouch Step – Right
23. Lift Sword and Kick with the Left Heel
24. Point Sword Down and Lift the Left Knee
25. Swing Sword in Crouch Step – left
26. Intercept Downward in Bow Step (Right and Left)
27. Thrust Sword Down in Bow Step
28. Cloud and Slide – Right and Left

29. Chop in Right Bow Step

30. Parry and Kick Backward

31. Point Sword Down in T-Step

32. Push Sword in Horse Step

Group 4

33. Lift Sword over Head in One Leg Standing

34. Step Up and Stab Back

35. Burst in Low Squat with Crossed Legs

36. Thrust Back in Bow Step

37. Turn Body Around and Thrust Down

38. Raise Sword with the Tip Down and Lift the Knee

39. Thrust and Marching

40. Parry with Lotus Kick

41. Thrust Straight in Bow Step

42. Closing

The features of Tai Chi sword

Will leads and the sword follows

Unify your body and the sword

Weaken the opposite's power and attack him in circles

Parry the attack and strike through the opening

Led by the waist

Deliver the energy through the sword

Perfect skill in a deft hand

Dignified and elegant

Power resides in the soft

Flexible and stable

Difficult to defend against and continuous

42式太極劍套路詳解

Analysis and Descriptions of the Movements of 42-form Tai Chi Sword

預備式

兩腳併攏，腳尖朝前；暢胸舒背，身體自然直立，兩臂自然垂於身體兩側，右手成劍指，手心朝裏；左手持劍，手心朝後，劍身豎直在左臂後面，劍尖向上，目視前方（圖2–1）

【要領】

頭頸自然豎直，下頷微收，上體保持自然，不可挺胸收腹。兩肩臂要自然鬆沉。劍刃不可觸及身體。精神要集中。

Preparation

Place the feet together, the toes pointing forward. Stretch the chest and back. Stand straight naturally. Both arms hang down at the sides of the body naturally. The right hand forms Sword Fingers, palm facing inward; the left hand holds the sword, palm facing back. Erect the blade of the sword behind the left arm, the tip pointing up. Eyes look ahead (Figure 2–1).

Key Points

Keep the head and the upper body upright naturally; the chin is tucked in slightly. Do not stiffen the chest or suck in the abdomen. The shoulders are naturally relaxed and sunken. Avoid touching the body with the edge of the sword. The mind is focused.

第一組

一、起　式

1. 左腳輕輕提起向左邁半步，與肩同寬，身體重心在兩腿中間。同時，兩臂微屈略內旋，兩手距身體約10公分，眼視前方（圖2-2）。

Group 1

1. Opening

(1) Lift the left foot gently to take a half step to the left. The feet are shoulder width apart. Shift the weight between the legs. Meanwhile, bend the arms and turn them inward slightly. The hands are about 10cm from the body. Eyes look ahead

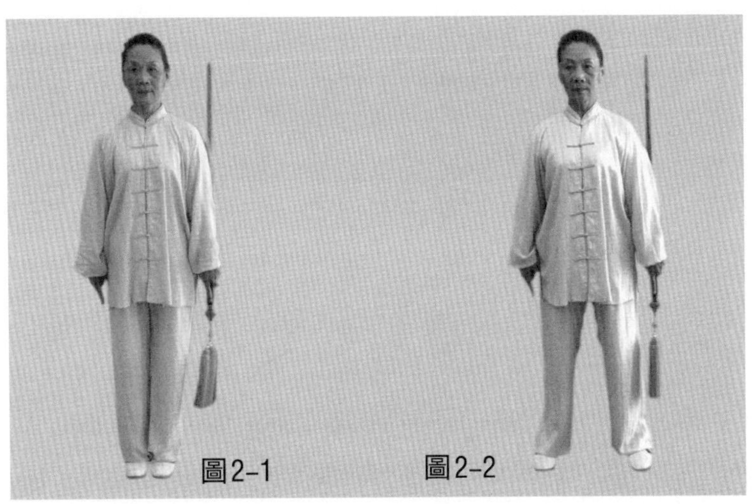

圖2-1　圖2-2

(Figure 2–2).

2. 兩臂自然伸直，隨上體微微左轉向左前擺舉至與肩平，手心朝下，劍身平貼於左小臂下，眼看左前方（圖2–3）。

(2) Extend the arms naturally. While turning the upper body to the left slightly, swing the arms to the left front at the level of the shoulder, palms facing down. The blade of the sword attaches to the underside of the left forearm. Eyes look to the left front (Figure 2–3).

3. 上體略右轉，隨轉體右手劍指右擺，至右前方後屈肘向下畫弧至腹前，手心向上；左手持劍，右擺後屈肘置於體前，腕與肩同高，手心向下，兩手心上下相對。同時，重心左移，左腿屈膝半蹲，右腳收提至左腳內側（腳不觸地），眼看右前方（圖2–4）。

(3) Turn the upper body to right slightly and swing the right Sword Fingers to the right front accordingly. Then bend the right elbow to draw an arc downward to the abdomen, palm facing up. Swing the left hand to the right and bend the elbow to move the sword in front of the body, the wrist at the level of the shoulders and palm facing down. Palms face each other. At the same time, shift the weight to the left and bend the left leg

in a half squat. Place the right foot beside the left foot (without touching the ground). Eyes look to the right front (Figure 2-4).

4. 右腳向右前方約45°上步，隨身體重心前移成右弓步。同時，右手劍指經左臂下向前上方擺舉，臂微屈，腕與肩同高，手心斜向上；左手持劍附於右前臂內側，劍柄在右前臂上方，手心向下，劍穗垂落於右前臂外側（圖2-5）。

(4) The right foot steps about to the right front 45° from the centre of the body. Shift the weight forward to form a Right Bow Step. Meanwhile, swing the right Sword Fingers from the underside of the left arm to the upper front, arm bent slightly, the wrist at shoulder level, and the palm facing diagonally up.

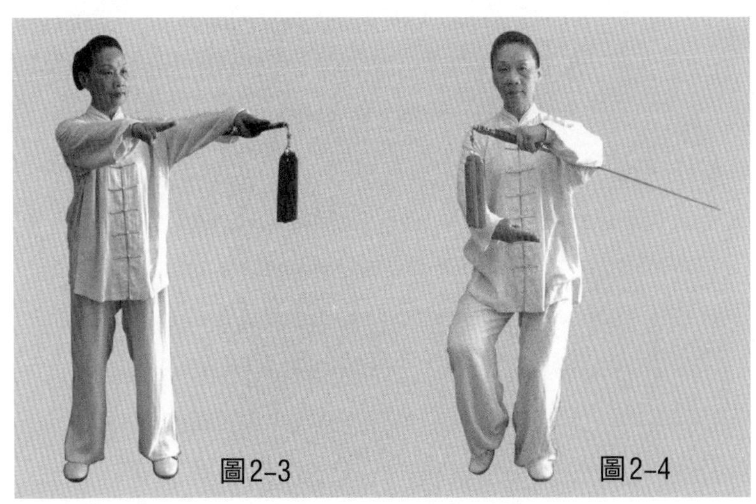

圖2-3 圖2-4

The left hand holds the sword and touches the inside of the right forearm. The handle is over the right forearm, the left palm facing down. The tassel of the sword hangs down at the outside of the right forearm (Figure 2–5).

5. 身體重心移於右腿，左腳跟至右腳內側後方，腳尖點地。同時，右手劍指向右前方伸送，左手持劍屈肘置於右胸前，手心向下，眼看劍指方向（圖2– 6）。

(5) Shift the weight onto the right leg. The left foot follows behind the inside of the right foot, only the toes touching the ground. Meanwhile, extend the right Sword Fingers to the right front and bend the left elbow in front of the right of the chest, palm facing down. Eyes look at the Sword Fingers (Figure 2–6).

圖2–5
圖2–6

6. 重心左移，右腳尖內扣，身體左轉約90°，左腳向左前方上步，成左弓步。同時，左手持劍經左膝前向左畫弧摟至左胯旁，臂微屈，手心向後，劍身豎直，劍尖朝上；右手劍指屈肘經右耳旁向前指出，手心斜向前，指尖向前上方，腕同肩高，眼看前方（圖2-7）。

（6）Shift the weight to the left. Turn the right toes inward and the body 90° to the left. The left foot takes a step to the left front, bending the leg to form a Left Bow Step. At the same time, the left hand holds the sword and draws an arc over the left knee to the side of the left hip, arm bent, palm facing the back. The blade of the sword is erected, the tip pointing up. Bend the right elbow and move the right Sword Fingers forward

圖2-7

from the side of the right ear, palm facing diagonally up, the fingertips pointing to the upper front, the wrist at shoulder level. Eyes look ahead (Figure 2-7).

【要領】

（1）兩手擺舉轉換要與重心移動協調配合，上體保持中正安舒，不可左右搖擺、前俯後仰。

（2）兩肩要鬆沉，胯部要沉，兩臂鬆舒，不可僵直，氣要下沉。

【攻防含義】

對方劍向我左腰部刺來，我則左手持劍，以劍摟擋對方劍，並近身上步，以劍指點擊對方喉部或雙眼。

Key Points

(1) The motions of hands are co-ordinated with the weight being shifted. Keep the upper body upright and comfortable. Do not sway to the left or right. Do not bend forward or backward.

(2) Keep the shoulders and arms relaxed. Sink the hips. Do not be stiff. Let the energy sink.

Application

When the opponent thrusts his sword towards to your left waist, hold your sword to parry it and step forward and wield your Sword Fingers out to stab his throat or eyes.

二、併步點劍

1. 重心前移，右腳經左腳內側向右前方約45°上步，隨重心前移成右弓步。同時，左手持劍經胸前向前穿出至右腕上，劍柄貼靠右腕（圖2-8）。

2. Point Sword Down and Feet Together

(1) Shift the weight forward. The right foot moves past the inside of the left foot, takes a step to the right front at about 45° from the centre of the body to form a Right Bow Step. Meanwhile, the left hand moves the sword forward across the chest and above the right wrist, with the grip of the sword touching the right wrist (Figure 2-8).

圖2-8

2. 上動不停，重心前移，左腳收提至右腳內側。同時，兩手分別向左右兩側擺舉後屈肘向下畫弧置於兩胯旁，手心均向下，眼看前方（圖2-9）。

(2) Shift the weight forward. Place the left foot beside the right foot. At the same time, swing the hands to the left and right respectively and draw arcs downward to the sides of the hip, palms facing down. Eyes look ahead (Figure 2-9).

3. 上體左轉，左腳向左前方約45°上步，隨重心前移成左弓步。同時，兩臂內旋，兩手分別向左右再向上向前畫弧於體前相合，左手在外，高與胸齊，手心向外，臂呈弧形，劍身貼靠左前臂，劍尖斜向後，右手虎口對劍柄準備接劍，眼看前方（圖2-10）。

(3) Turn the upper body to the left. The left foot takes a step about 45° to the left front. Shift the weight forward to form a Left Bow Step. Meanwhile, rotate the arms inward and move the hands respectively to the right and left then both upward and forward in arcs to join together in front of the body. The left hand is on the outside of the right hand at the height of the waist, palm facing outward and the arm arched. The blade of the sword is attached to the left forearm, the tip pointing diagonally back. Put the right "tiger mouth" (the part between the thumb and the first finger) against the hilt, ready to take over

the sword. Eyes look ahead (Figure 2-10).

4. 身體重心前移，右腳向左腳併步，並屈膝半蹲。同時，右手接握劍柄，隨以腕關節為軸，使劍尖由身體左後方向上向前畫弧，至腕與胸同高時，提腕使劍尖向前下方點劍，左手變劍指附於右腕內側，眼看劍尖（圖2-11）。

(4) Shift the weight forward. Place the right foot close to the left foot and bend the knees in a half squat. Meanwhile, the right hand takes over the sword. Use the right wrist as the axle, the tip of the sword draws an arc from the left back of the body to the upper front. When the wrist reaches the height of the chest, lift the wrist to point the sword to the lower front.

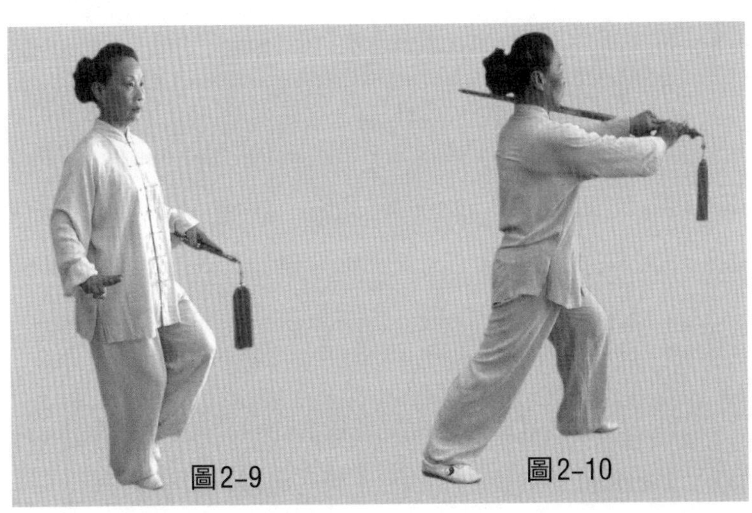

圖2-9 圖2-10

The left hand turns into Sword Fingers and touches the inside of the right wrist. Eyes look at the tip of the sword (Figure 2-11).

【要領】

（1）兩手側分擺舉畫弧與弓步要協調一致，兩臂不要僵挺；右手接劍時動作要自然，不要停頓。

（2）點劍時，上體保持正直，要鬆肩、鬆腰、沉胯、斂臀。不可聳肩、拱背或突臀。手腕要先下沉後上提，沉吸提呼，勁注劍尖。

【攻防含義】

對方伏身以劍刺我小腿，我則以劍點擊對方腕部。

Key Points

(1) The separation of the hands should be coordinated with the Bow Step. The arms should not be rigid. The right hand takes over the sword naturally without pause.

(2) When pointing the sword down, keep the upper body upright. Relax the shoulders and the waist. Sink the hips. Pull the buttocks in. Do not lift the shoulders, stoop, or push the buttocks out. Sink the wrist first and then lift it; sink while inhaling and lift while exhaling. Deliver the force to the tip of the sword.

Application

When the opponent lowers his body to attack your lower legs, you point the sword to attack the opponent's wrist.

三、弓步削劍

1. 身體重心移至左腿，右腳跟提起。同時，右手握劍沉腕，手心翻向上，使劍尖畫一小弧向左下方；左手劍指附於右前臂內側，手心向右，指尖向上，眼看劍尖方向（圖2-12）。

3. Peel in Bow Step

(1) Shift the weight onto the left leg. Lift the right heel off the ground. Meanwhile, the right hand holds the sword, sinking the wrist and turning over the palm to face up. Move the tip of the sword in a small arc to the lower left. The left Sword Fingers attach to the inside of the right forearm, palm facing the

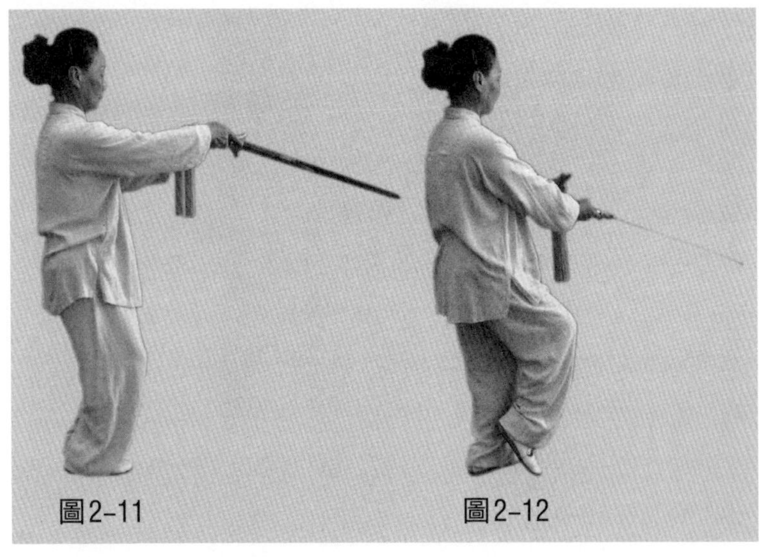

圖2-11　圖2-12

right and the fingertips pointing up. Eyes look at the tip of the sword (Figure 2–12).

2. 右腳向右後方撤步，腳跟著地，上體重心右移，左腳尖內扣，右腳尖外展，右腿屈膝前弓，成右弓步。同時，右手握劍隨轉體向右上方斜削，腕同肩高；左手劍指左擺置於左胯旁，手心斜向下，指尖向前，眼看劍尖方向（圖2–13）。

(2) The right foot steps to the right back, only the heel touching the ground. Shift the weight to the right. Swing the left toes inward and the right toes outward. Bend the knee forward to form a Right Bow Step. Meanwhile, following the body turn, peel to the right with the blade slanted and the wrist at shoul–

圖2–13

der level. Move the left Sword Fingers to the side of the left hip, palm facing down, the fingertips pointing the front. Eyes look at the tip of the sword (Figure 2–13).

【要領】

(1) 上體右轉成右弓步和斜削劍方向一致，與併步點劍方向相反。

(2) 斜削劍要與轉腰、弓步協調一致，以腰帶臂，使勁力達劍刃前端。上體中正，神態自然，不可彎腰擺頭。

【攻防含義】

若對方以劍從我右後方刺我頭部，我則以劍前端拇指一側劍刃從對方劍下向其頸部削去。

Key Points

(1) The Right Bow Step points the same direction as the sword and opposite with the pointing direction of the sword in "Point Sword Down and Feet Together".

(2) The peeling action should be coordinated with the turning waist and the Bow Step. Use the waist to lead the arm and deliver the force to the front part of the sword. Keep the upper body upright and the manner natural. Do not stoop or sway the head.

Application

If the opponent thrust your head from your right back, you can use the front edge of the sword on the thumb side to peel towards the opponent's neck.

四、提膝劈劍

1. 左腿屈膝，上體重心後移並略向右轉，右腳尖蹺起外擺。同時，右手握劍屈肘向右向後畫弧至上體右後方，手心向上，腕略高於腰；左手劍指向前向右畫弧擺至右肩前，手心斜向下，眼隨劍走（圖2-14）。

4. Chop and Lift the Knee

(1) Bend the left leg. Shift the weight backward and turn the body to the right slightly. Lift the right toes and turn them

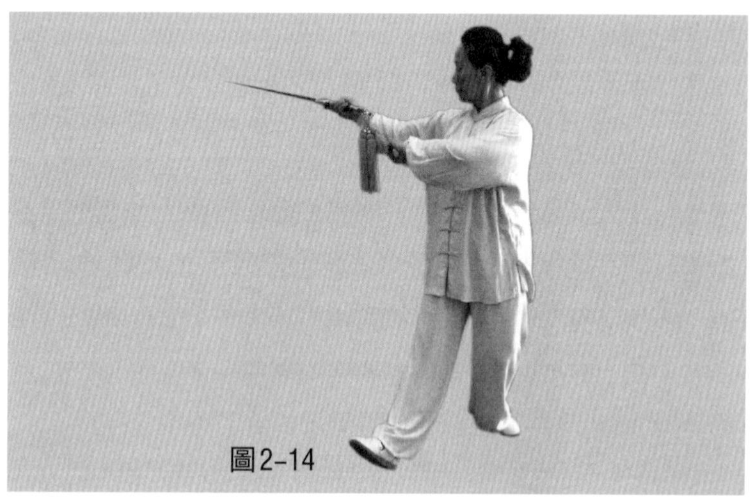
圖2-14

outward. Meanwhile, the right hand holds the sword with the elbow bent, and draws an arc to the right back of the upper body, palm facing up and the wrist slightly higher than the waist. The left Sword Fingers move forward first then to the right in an arc in front of the right shoulder, palm facing diagonally down. Eyes follow the sword (Figure 2-14).

2. 上體微向左轉，重心前移，右腳踏實，右腿隨重心前移自然直立，左腿屈膝提起成右獨立步。同時，右手握劍向上向前平劈，左手劍指往下向左畫弧擺舉至與肩平，手心向外，指尖向前，眼看劍尖（圖2-15）。

(2) Turn the upper body to the left slightly. While shifting the weight forward, the right foot steps on the ground solidly

圖2-15

and stands straight naturally. Bend the left leg and lift it to form a Right One Leg Stand. At the meantime, the right hand holds the sword to chop upward and forward, with the tip at shoulder level. The left Sword Fingers move downward and leftward to draw an arc to the level of the shoulders, palm facing outward, the fingertips pointing forward. Eyes look at the tip of the sword (Figure 2–15).

【要領】

（1）上體左右轉動要與兩臂動作協調一致。提膝獨立要與劈劍協調一致。勁貫劍身下刃。

（2）獨立劈劍提膝不可低於腰，右腿站立要平穩。兩臂同高，夾角不小於90°。劈劍時，劍與臂要平直一線。

（3）重心後移時，要收臀，收腹，屈髖，上體保持正直舒鬆，不可後仰。

【攻防含義】

若對方以劍刺我頭部，我則以劍身帶化開其來劍，隨即立劍劈向對方頭部。

Key Points

(1) Turning the upper body showld be coordinated with moving the arms. So is lifting the leg with chopping. The force goes through the lower edge of the sword.

(2) Lift the knee higher than the waist. The right leg stands steadily. The arms are at the same level and form an angle over 90° . While chopping, the sword is on a line with the arm.

(3) When shifting the weight backward, draw the hip in and hold in the abdomen. Keep the upper body upright and re-laxed. Do not bend backward.

Application

If the opponent thrusts your head with a sword, you can deflect it away with the blade of your sword, and then hold the sword with its edge up to chop towards the opponent's head.

五、左弓步攔

1. 右腿屈膝半蹲，上體左轉，左腳向左後落步，腳前掌著地。同時，右手握劍以腕關節為軸，使劍尖在體前順時針畫一弧，置於身體右前方；左手劍指右擺，屈肘附於右前臂內側，手心向下，眼看劍尖方向（圖2-16）。

5. Parry in Left Bow Step

(1) Bend the right leg in a half squat. Turn the upper body to the left. The left foot takes a step to the left back, only the forefoot touching the ground. At the same time, the right hand, using the wrist as the axle, draws an arc clockwise with the tip of sword in front of the body and stops at the right front.

The left Sword Fingers swing to the right and attach to the inside of the right forearm, elbow bent and palm facing down. Eyes look at the tip of the sword (Figure 2-16).

2. 上體左轉約90°，重心向左腿移動，右腳尖內扣，左腳尖外擺，左腿屈膝成左弓步。同時，右手握劍，隨轉體經下向左前方畫弧攔出，手心斜向上，腕與頭同高，小指側劍刃向上，劍尖向前下；左手劍指經下向左向上畫弧，臂呈弧形舉於頭左前上方，手心斜向上，眼看劍尖方向（圖2-17）。

(2) Turn the upper body about 90° to the left. Shift the

圖2-16
圖2-17

weight onto the left leg. Turn the right toes inward and the left toes outward. Bend the left knee to form a Left Bow Step. Meanwhile, following the body turn, wield the sword in an arc to the left front to parry the opponent's sword, palm facing diagonally up and wrist at the height of the head. The edge of the sword on the little finger side faces up, the tip pointing to the lower front. The left Sword Fingers move to the left and then upward in an arc to the upper left front of the head, arm arched and palm facing diagonally up. Eyes look at the tip of the sword (Figure 2–17).

【要領】

（1）上體轉動與劍繞環要協調一致，以腰帶臂攔劍。

（2）弓步時上體不可前俯，攔劍時上體正直，不可向右彎腰擺頭。

【攻防含義】

若對方劍向我左側方刺來，則我以劍身中部攔擋其劍。

Key Points

(1) Turning the upper body should be coordinated with moving the sword in an arc. Use the waist to drive the arm parrying.

(2) In the Bow Step, do not bend forward. While parrying

with the sword, keep the upper body upright. Do not bend the waist to the right or sway the head.

Application

If the opponent's sword stabs your left side, you can parry it with the middle part of the blade of your sword.

六、左虛步撩

1. 上體左轉，重心後移，右腿屈膝，左腳尖蹺起並稍外展；而後，隨重心前移左腳落地踏實，上體稍右轉，右腳向右前方上步，腳跟著地。同時，右手握劍隨轉體屈肘向上向左畫弧至左胯旁，手心向裏，劍尖斜朝後上方，左手劍指下落附於右腕處，眼看劍尖方向（圖2-18）。

6. Upward Slice in Left Empty Step

(1) Turn the upper body to the left. Shift the weight backward. Bend the right knee. Lift the left toes and turn it slightly outward. Shifting the weight forward, place the left foot on the ground solidly. Turn the upper body slightly to the right. The right foot takes a step to the right front, only the heel touching the ground. At the meantime, bend the right elbow and wield the sword upward and leftward drawing an arc to the outside of the left hip, palm facing inward, and the tip pointing to the upper back. Place the left Sword Fingers onto the right wrist. Eyes

look at the tip of the sword (Figure 2–18).

2. 上體右轉不停，右腳尖外展，隨重心前移右腳尖落地，全腳踏實，右腿屈膝半蹲，左腳向左前方上步成左虛步。同時，右手握劍，劍刃領先經後向下向左前上方立圓撩架至頭前上方，臂微屈，手心向外，劍尖略低，左手劍指附於右腕處，眼看左前方（圖2–19）。

(2) Continue to turn the upper body to the right. Turn the right toes outward, shifting the weight forward, and place the entire foot on the ground firmly. Bend the right knee in a half squat and the left foot takes a step to the left front to form a Left Empty Step. Meanwhile, with the edge ahead, move the sword backward first and then to the upper left front to draw a

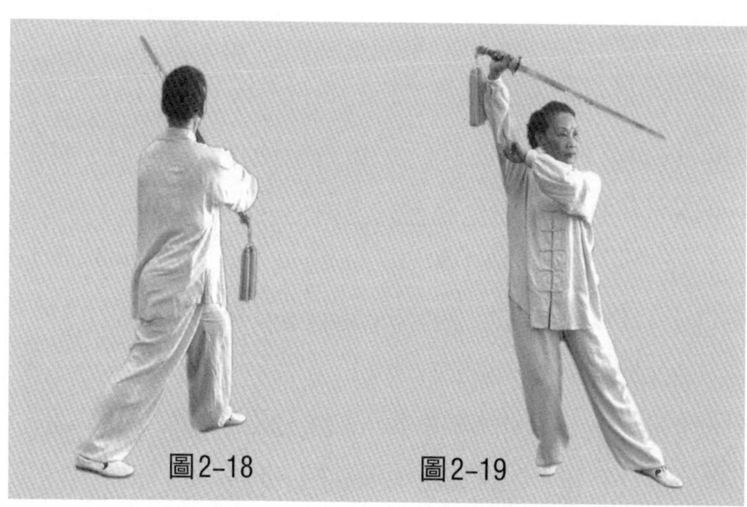
圖2–18 圖2–19

vertical arc to the upper front of the head, arm arched slightly and palm facing outward, the tip is slightly lower than the blade. The left Sword Fingers stay on the right wrist. Eyes look to the left front (Figure 2–19).

【要領】

（1）劍向左後繞環要與上體轉換協調一致，向前撩劍要與邁左步協調一致。整個動作要連貫圓活。

（2）撩劍方向偏右30°，撩劍劍尖不宜過低，力達劍刃前端。

【攻防含義】

若對方以劍刺我右腰部，我右轉上步閃身後，提腕以劍小指側刃前端由下向上撩擊對方腕部。

Key Points

(1) Drawing the arc with the sword should be coordinated with the turning of the body. The slicing should be coordinated with the step to the left. The entire movement should be continuous and fluent.

(2) Slice the sword 30° to the right. The tip should not be too lower. Deliver the force to the front part of the edge.

Application

If the opponent uses the sword to attack your right waist, you can turn right and step forward to dodge it, then lift the wrist and wield the sword upward to attack the opponent's wrist with the front part of the edge on the little finger side.

七、右弓步撩

1. 身體微右轉，左腳向左上步，腳跟著地。同時，右手握劍落至身體右上方，腕稍低於肩，臂微屈，劍尖朝右上方；左手劍指屈肘落於右肩前，手心斜向下，眼看劍尖方向（圖2-20）。

7. Upward Slice in Right Bow Step

(1) Turn the body to the right slightly. The left foot steps to the left, only the heel touching the ground. Meanwhile, the right hand moves the sword to the upper right of the body with the wrist slightly lower than the shoulders, arm slightly bent,

圖2-20

and the tip pointing the upper right. Bend the left elbow and place the left Sword Fingers in front of the right shoulder, palm facing diagonally down. Eyes look at the tip of the sword (Figure 2-20).

2. 上體左轉，左腳尖外展，重心向左腳移，左腳踏實，隨即右腳向前上步，隨重心前移成右弓步。同時，右手握劍經下向前立劍撩出，腕同肩高，手心斜向上，劍尖斜向下；左手劍指向下向左上方畫弧，臂呈弧形舉於頭左上方，手心斜朝上，眼看劍尖方向（圖2-21）。

(2) Turn the upper body to the left. Turn the left toes outward. While shifting the weight onto the left foot, place the left

圖2-21

foot on the ground solidly. Then the right foot takes a step forward. Shift the weight forward to form a Right Bow Step. Meanwhile, the right hand holds the sword to slice upward with the edge up, the tip pointing diagonally down, the wrist at shoulder level, the palm facing diagonally up. The left Sword Fingers draw an arc to the upper left of the head, arm arched and palm facing diagonally up. Eyes look at the tip of the sword (Figure 2-21).

【要領】

（1）撩劍時，劍要貼身立圓撩出，幅度要大，動作要做到勢動神隨；上步時重心要平穩，不可起伏。

（2）左臂要撐圓，肘部不可屈折，撩劍的右臂要微屈，腕部上凸，劍尖不要過低，力達劍身前端。

【攻防含義】

若對方以劍向我左肋部刺來，我進步左轉身避開其來劍，隨即以劍小指側刃由下向上撩擊對方腕部。

Key Points

(1) While slicing up, wield the sword in a large vertical ellipse close to the body. The eyes follow the sword. Keep the weight stable while stepping forward; do not move it up or down.

(2) The left arm is arched. Do not form an angle at the elbow. When it is time to slice up, bend the right arm slightly and lift the wrist. The tip of the sword should not be too low. Deliver the force to the front part of the blade.

Application

If the opponent uses the sword to attack your left ribs, you can step forward and turn to the left to dodge it, and then slice towards the opponent's wrist with the edge of the sword on the little finger side.

八、提膝捧劍

1. 左腿屈膝半蹲，重心後移，身體略向左轉。同時，右手握劍隨轉體向左平帶，手心向上，腕同胸高，劍尖向前；左手劍指屈肘下落附於右腕處，手心向下，眼看劍尖方向（圖2-22）。

8. Hold Sword with Both Hands and Lift the Knee

(1) Bend the left leg in a half squat. Shift the weight backward. Turn the body to the left slightly. Meanwhile, following the body, withdraw the sword to the left horizontally, palm facing up, the wrist at chest level, and the tip of the sword pointing forward. Place the left Sword Fingers on the right wrist, palm facing downward. Eyes look at the tip of the sword (Figure 2-22).

2. 上體略向右轉，右腳向後撤步，隨重心後移成左虛步。同時，右手握劍隨轉體手心轉向下，使劍經體前向右平帶至右胯旁，劍尖朝前；左手劍指向下向左畫弧至左胯旁，手心朝下，眼看劍尖方向（圖2-23）。

(2) Turn the upper body to the right slightly. The right foot steps back. Shift the weight backward to form a Left Empty Step. Meanwhile, turn over the right hand to make the palm face down and withdraw the sword horizontally to the right side of the hip, the tip pointing forward. The left Sword Fingers move downward and to the left in an arc to the side of the left hip, palm facing down. Eyes look at the tip of the sword (Figure 2-23).

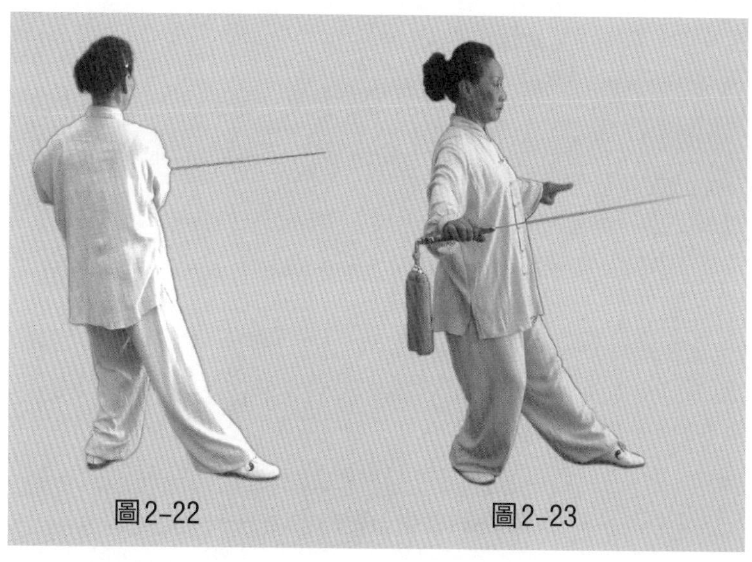
圖2-22　圖2-23

3. 左腳向前活步，隨重心前移，左腿自然直立，右腿屈膝提起成左獨立步。同時，兩手手心翻轉朝上隨提膝由兩側向胸前相合，左手劍指捧托右手背下，與胸同高，劍尖向前，略高於腕，眼看前方（圖2-24）。

(3) The left foot makes Moving Steps forward. While shifting the weight forward, the left leg stands straight naturally. Bend the right knee and lift it to form a One Leg Stand. Meanwhile, both hands turn over so that the palms face up and move to join together in front of the chest. The left Sword Fingers hold the back of the right hand at chest level. The tip of sword points forward and higher than the wrist slightly. Eyes look ahead (Figure 2-24).

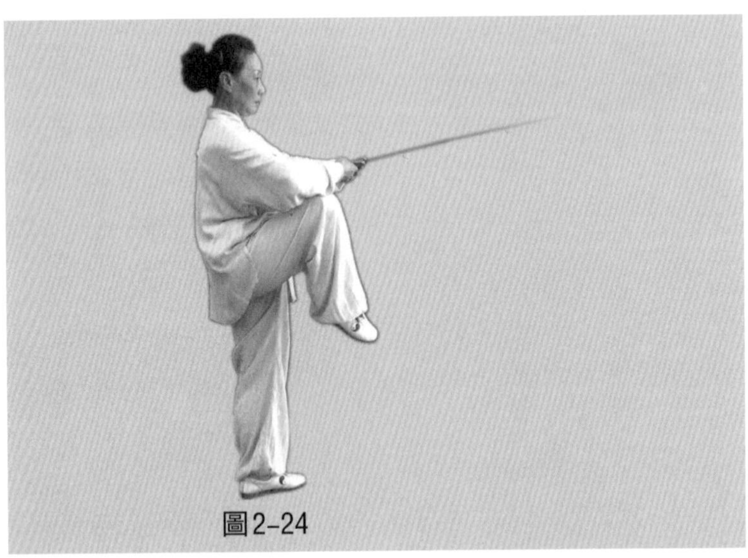

圖2-24

【要領】

（1）左右轉體帶劍要協調連貫；提膝與捧劍協調一致；提膝不低於腰部。

（2）捧劍時，左手可是劍指，也可為掌。

（3）左右平帶劍時，劍尖要對準身體中心線。

【攻防含義】

若對方劍向我胸部刺來，我由下向上捧起劍，托化對方來劍。

Key Points

(1) Turning the body and withdrawing the sword should be continuous and coordinated with each other. The same applies to the actions of lifting the knee and holding the sword. The lifted knee should not be lower than the waist.

(2) When holding the sword with both hands, the left hand can be the form of either a Sword Fingers or an open palm.

(3) When withdrawing the sword to the right or left, keep the tip aligned with the centre of the body.

Application

If the opponent uses a sword to attack your chest, you can hold the sword upward to parry this attack.

九、蹬腳前刺

左腳直立站穩，右腳以腳跟為力點，腳尖勾回向前用力蹬出。同時，兩手捧劍略向下回引再向上向前平刺，眼看劍尖方向（圖2-25）。

【要領】

（1）蹬腳須以腳跟為力點，勾腳蹬出不得低於腰；頭要虛領，上體正直，不可前俯或挺腹。

（2）捧劍回引時，左腿微屈再伸直，使上體下沉再上升，與蹬腳和前刺協調一致。

（3）劍向前平刺時，兩臂保持鬆沉。

【攻防含義】

若對方用劍向我胸部刺來，我以劍壓對方來劍再向對方喉部刺去。

9. Thrust Forward and Kick with the Heel

The left leg stands straight and steadily. Kick forward with

圖2-25

the right foot forcefully, force on the heel, the toes pointing back. Meanwhile, the hands hold the sword to move slightly downward first, then upward in an arc, and then thrust it forward. Eyes look at the tip of the sword (Figure 2-25).

Key Points

(1) When kicking out, the force is on the heel, which is higher than the waist. Draw the head up naturally and keep the upper body upright. Do not bend forward or push out the abdomen.

(2) When moving the sword backward, bend the left leg slightly first and then extend it straight, to make the upper body sink first and then rise up, coordinated with the kicking and thrusting.

(3) When thrusting the sword forward, keep the shoulders relaxed and sunken.

Application

If the opponent uses a sword to attack your chest, you can use your sword to push against it and then thrust it towards the opponent's throat.

十、跳步平刺

1. 右腳向前落步，隨身體重心前移右腳蹬地，頭上領，左腳腳面展平提起後擺。同時，兩手捧劍向前刺去，眼看前方（圖2-26）。

10. Jump and Thrust Flat

(1) The right foot steps forward. While shifting the weight forward, push the ground with the right foot, draw the head up, and swing the left foot backward with the sole extended. Meanwhile, both hands hold the sword to thrust forward. Eyes look ahead (Figure 2–26).

2. 右腳蹬地、頭上領的同時，後擺左腳向前躍步落地踏實，腿微屈；右腳在左腳落地的同時迅速向左腳內側靠攏，腳尖不點地。兩手同時內旋撤於兩胯旁，手心均向下，右手持劍平置，眼看前方（圖2–27）。

圖2–26
圖2–27

(2) With the right foot pushing against the ground, the left foot jumps forward and steps on the ground solidly, leg slightly bent. As the left foot touches the ground, move the right foot rapidly to the inside of the left foot without touching the ground with the toes. Meanwhile, turn both hands inward and separate them apart to the sides of the hip, palms facing down. The right hand is holding the sword with the blade flat. Eyes look ahead (Figure 2-27).

3. 右腳向前上步成右弓步。同時，右手握劍經腰部向前平刺，腕同胸高，手心向上，勁注劍尖；左手劍指經左向上向前畫弧，臂呈弧形舉於頭左上方，手心斜向上，眼看劍尖方向（圖2-28）。

圖2-28

(3) The right foot takes a step forward to form a Right Bow Step. Meanwhile, the right hand holds the sword and thrusts it forward from the waist, the wrist at chest level and palm facing up. Deliver the force to the tip of the sword. The left Sword Fingers move upward then forward in an arc to the upper left of the head, arm arched and palm facing diagonally up. Eyes look at the tip of the sword (Figure 2-28).

【要領】

(1) 跳步時，要向前移重心再落步蹬地，動作要自然、輕靈，並要有一定距離。跨步不宜太小。

(2) 跳步時，身體不要上竄，跳步後，左前腳掌先著地後全腳踩實踩穩，右腳速收於左腳內側，稍停頓再上步刺。

(3) 右腳落步與前刺，左跳步與兩手回抽要協調一致。

【攻防含義】

上動我向對方喉部刺去，對方低頭閃身向我胸部刺來，我則跳步近身以劍壓化對方之劍，再乘機上步刺擊對方胸部。

Key Points

(1) When jumping, shift the weight forward first and then step on the ground and push against it. The motion should be

light, gentle and natural. The jump step should not be short.

(2) While jumping, do not move the body up. After the jump, place the left forefoot on the ground first and then the entire foot on the ground firmly. The right foot moves back to the inside of the left foot quickly. After a short pause, the right foot steps forward to thrust the sword forward.

(3) The right foot falling on the ground and the sword being thrust forward are coordinated with each other. The same applies to the jump and pulling back the hands.

Application

Following the last movement, when you thrust your sword to the opponent's throat, the opponent would lower his head and move aside to thrust his sword towards your chest. At the time, you can jump forward to close to him and push against his sword with yours, and then take the chance to step forward and stab his chest.

十一、轉身下刺

1. 左腿屈膝，重心後移；右腿自然伸直，腳尖上蹺。同時，右手握劍向左向後平帶屈肘收至胸前，手心向上；左手劍指屈肘置於胸前，劍身平貼於左前臂下，兩手心斜相對，眼看左前方（圖2-29）。

11. Turn Body and Thrust Down

(1) Bend the left leg. Shift the weight backward. Extend the right leg naturally straight and lift the toes up. Meanwhile, the right hand moves the sword to the left then backward with its blade flat and draws it back in front of the chest by bending the elbow, palm facing up. Bend the left arm in front of the chest. The blade of the sword clings to the underside of the left forearm. The palms diagonally face to each other. Eyes look to the left front (Figure 2–29).

2. 右腳尖內扣落地，重心移至右腿；而後以右腳掌為軸，身體左後轉270°；左腿屈膝提起收至右腳內側，腳不著地。兩手仍合於胸前，眼看左前方（圖2–30）。

圖2–29 圖2–30

(2) Swing the right toes inward and place the entire foot on the ground. Shift the weight onto the right leg. Pivoting on the right forefoot, turn the body about 270° to the left. Bend the left leg and place the foot beside the right foot without touching the ground. Both hands stay in their positions. Eyes look to the left front (Figure 2–30).

3. 左腳向左前方落步，成左弓步。同時，右手握劍向左前下方平劍刺出，手心向上；左手劍指向左向上畫弧，臂呈弧形，舉於頭前左上方，手心斜向上，眼看劍尖方向（圖2–31）。

(3) The left foot takes a step to the left front to form a Left Bow Step. At the same time, thrust the sword to the lower

圖2–31

left front, with the blade flat and palm facing up. The left Sword Fingers moves in an arc to the upper left front of the head, arm arched and palm facing diagonally up. Eyes look at the tip of the sword (Figure 2-31).

【要領】

(1) 轉身下刺，轉體時左腳蹬地，以右腳掌為軸轉動，上體正直、舒鬆，頭要領起，重心平穩。

(2) 支撐腿微屈，降低重心，落步與刺劍要協調一致。

【攻防含義】

若上動未能刺擊對方，對方向右方避開，我將轉身上步向對方膝部刺去。

Key Points

(1) While turning the body, the left foot pushes against the ground. When pivoting on the right forefoot, keep the upper body upright and relaxed. Draw the head up and keep the weight steady.

(2) Bend the supporting leg slightly. Lower the weight. Placing the left foot on the ground should be coordinated with thrusting the sword.

Application

If you did not succeed in attacking the opponent in the

last movement and the opponent dodges away to the right, you can turn the body and step forward to thrust your sword towards the opponent's knee.

第二組

十二、弓步平斬

1. 重心前移，右腳收於左腳內側，不著地。同時，右手握劍，沉腕，手心斜向上，左手劍指屈肘向前附於右前臂上，眼看劍尖（圖2-32）。

Group 2

12. Horizontal Slash in Bow Step

(1) Shift the weight forward. The right foot moves to the

圖2-32

inside of the left foot without touching the ground. Meanwhile, the right hand holds the sword, wrist sunken and palm facing diagonally up. Bend the left arm and rest the left Sword Fingers on the right forearm. Eyes look at the tip of the sword (Figure 2–32).

2. 右腳向右後方撤步，左腳碾步內扣成右橫襠步，身體右轉約90°。同時，右手握劍向右平斬，左手劍指向左分展側舉，略低於胸，手心向左，指尖向前，眼看劍尖（圖2–33）。

(2) The right foot steps to the right back. Pivot on the left heel inward to form a right Side Bow Step. Turn the body about 90° to the right. Meanwhile, the right hand wields the sword,

圖2–33

slashing to the right with its blade flat. Extend the left arm and lift the Sword Fingers to the left and slightly lower than the chest, palm facing the left and the fingertips pointing forward. Eyes look at the tip of the sword (Figure 2–33).

【要領】

肩、肘鬆活，以腰帶臂，眼隨劍走，運勁沉穩不斷。

【攻防含義】

若對方向我右腰部刺來，我收腳閃身，上步右轉身，以劍拇指一側刃斬向對方腰部。

Key Points

Keep the shoulders and elbows relaxed and flexible. Use the waist to lead the shoulders. Eyes follow the sword. Deliver the energy steadily and continuously.

Application

If the opponent attacks your waist, you can avoid it by bringing in the foot and moving aside. Then step forward and turn to the right slashing towards the opponent's waist with the edge of the sword on the thumb's side.

十三、弓步崩劍

1. 重心左移，上體略左轉。隨轉體右手握劍，以劍柄領先，屈肘向左帶劍至面前，手心向後；左手劍指弧形左擺至左胯旁，手心向下，指尖向前，眼向右看（圖2-34）。

13. Burst in Bow Step

(1) Shift the weight to the left. Turn the upper body to the left slightly. Following the body, bend the right arm to move the sword to the right with its handle ahead and stop in front of the head, palm facing back. The left Sword Fingers draw an arc to the left hip, palm facing down and the fingertips pointing the front. Eyes look to the right (Figure 2-34).

2. 重心右移，左腳經右腳後向右插步成叉步。同時，右手劍略向左帶後內旋翻，手心向下，向右格

圖2-34

帶，腕同胸高，手臂自然伸直，劍尖向前，同肩高；左手劍指向左擺舉，腕同肩高，手心向外，指尖向前，眼向右看（圖2-35）。

(2) Shift the weight to the right. The left foot moves to the right back of the right foot to form a Crossover Backward Step. Meanwhile, the right hand moves the sword to the left slightly and turns over, palm facing down. Then bring the sword to the right with the arm stretched naturally, wrist at chest level. The tip of the sword points forward at the shoulders level. The left Sword Fingers swing to the left, wrist at the height of the shoulder, palm facing outward and the fingertips pointing forward. Eyes look to the right (Figure 2-35).

圖2-35

3. 重心移至左腿，右腿屈膝提起。同時，兩臂內旋，兩手合於腹前，手心向上，劍尖向前，左手劍指捧托於右手背下，眼看前方（圖2-36）。

(3) Shift the weight onto the left leg. Bend the right leg and lift it. Meanwhile, both arms turn inward and the hands join together in front of the abdomen, palms facing up and the tip of the sword pointing forward. The left Sword Fingers hold the back of the right hand. Eyes look ahead (Figure 2-36).

4. 右腳向右落步成右弓步，上體略右轉。同時，右手握劍右擺崩劍，勁貫劍身前端，腕同肩高，劍尖高於腕，臂微屈，手心向上；左手劍指向左分展，停於左胯旁，手心向下，眼看劍尖（圖2-37）。

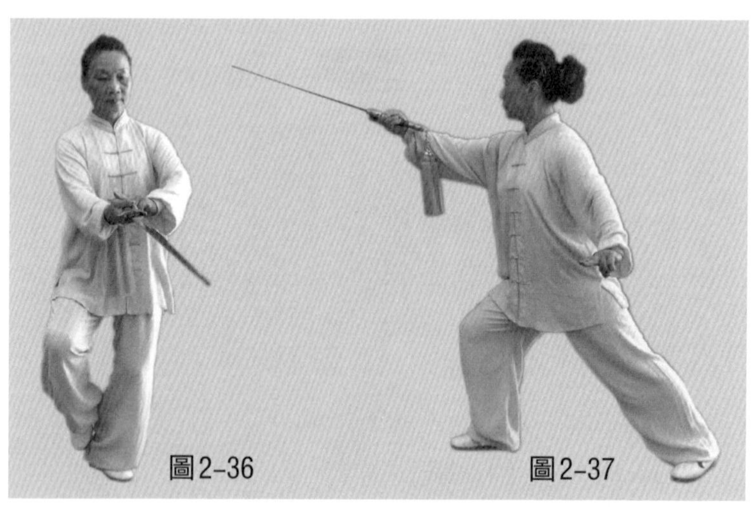
圖2-36　圖2-37

(4) The right foot steps to the right to form a Right Bow Step. Turn the upper body to the right slightly. Meanwhile, swing the sword to the right and tilt the tip of the sword up, delivering the force to the front part of its blade, the wrist at the level of the shoulder, arm bent slightly and palm facing up. The tip of the sword is higher than the wrist. The left Sword Fingers move to the left and stop at the left hip, palm facing down. Eyes look at the tip of the sword (Figure 2-37).

【要領】

(1)捧劍與提膝，崩劍與弓步要協調一致。

(2)崩劍要沉胯，吸氣蓄勁，轉腰發勁；發勁要鬆彈，動作要連貫，一氣呵成。

【攻防含義】

若對方用劍向我右腰側或下盤刺來，我右轉身閃開其劍，左腳蹬地轉腰發勁，以劍上鋒崩擊對方頸或頭。

Key Points

(1) Holding the sword and lifting the knee are coordinated with each other. The same applies to tilting the sword and the Bow Step.

(2) When tilting the sword, sink the hip and inhale to accumulate power. Turn the waist to release the power, loose and elastic. The movement should be continuous and finished as a

whole.

Application

If the opponent uses a sword to thrust towards your right waist or lower body, you can turn to the right to dodge it, and then with your left foot pushing the ground, turn the waist to release power and to attack the opponent's head or neck with the upper edge of your sword.

十四、歇步壓劍

1. 上體左轉，重心移至左腿，右腳向左腳後插步。同時，右手握劍內旋提腕向上向左畫弧，手心向下，左手劍指上舉至與肩同高，眼看右手（圖2-38）。

圖2-38

14. Pressing Sword in Low Squat with Crossing Legs

(1) Turn the body to the left. Shift the weight onto the left leg. The right foot steps to the left back of the left foot to form Crossover Backward Step. At the same time, turn the right hand inward and lift the wrist to move the sword to the upper left in an arc, palm facing down. Raise the left Sword Fingers to shoulder level. Eyes look at the right hand (Figure 2–38).

2. 兩腿屈膝下蹲成歇步。同時，右手握劍下壓，臂微屈，腕與膝同高；左手劍指向上畫弧，臂呈弧形舉於頭左側上方，手心斜向上，眼看劍尖（圖2–39）。

(2) Bend the legs in a Low Squat with Crossover Legs.

圖2–39

Meanwhile, the right hand presses the sword downward, arm bent and the wrist at knee level. The left Sword Fingers draw an arc to the upper left of the head with the arm arched, palm facing diagonally up. Eyes look at the tip of the sword (Figure 2–39).

【要領】

（1）壓劍時，以劍脊為力點，肩、肘鬆沉，起落矯健，不可僵直。

（2）劍身與地面平行，方向偏左前方30°，劍身距地面約10公分。

【攻防含義】

若對方劍從我左前向我腰下部刺來，我轉身用劍下壓對方來劍。

Key Points

(1) When pressing the sword downward, deliver the force to the spine. Keep the shoulders and elbows relaxed and sunken. Move nimbly and forcefully. Do not be rigid.

(2) Hold the sword with its blade at the height of 10cm and parallel to the ground, pointing about 30° to the left front.

Application

If the opponent attacks your lower waist from the left front, you can turn body and push against his sword with your sword.

十五、進步絞劍

1. 上體略右轉，兩腿蹬伸，左腿屈膝，右腳向前上步成右虛步。同時，右手握劍虎口向前上方立劍上提，腕與肩同高，劍尖略低於腕；左手劍指經上弧形前擺，附於右前臂內側，手心向下，眼看前下方（圖2–40）。

15. Stirring and Marching

(1) Turn the upper body to the right slightly. Extend the legs. Bend the left knee and move the right foot forward to form a Right Empty Step. Meanwhile, hold the sword with the edge up and lift it with the "Tiger Mouth" facing the upper front, wrist at the shoulder level and the tip slightly lower than the

圖2–40

wrist. Swing the left Sword Fingers upward in an arc to the inside of the right forearm, palm facing down. Eyes look to the lower front (Figure 2–40).

2. 右腳向前上步，重心前移。同時，右手握劍絞劍，左手劍指向下向左畫弧側舉，腕略高於肩，手心向外，指尖向前，臂呈弧形，眼看劍尖前方（圖2–41）。

(2) The right foot takes a step forward. Shift the weight forward. Meanwhile, the right hand makes a stirring motion with the sword. The left Sword Fingers move downward then to the left then upward in an arc, wrist slightly higher than the shoulder, arm arched, palm facing outward and the fingertips

圖2–41

pointing the front. Eyes look at the tip of the sword (Figure 2–41).

3. 左腳輕提向前上步，重心前移。同時，右手握劍再次絞劍，左手劍指動作不變，向後撐勁，眼看劍尖（圖2–42）。

(3) Lift the left foot gently and move it one step forward. Shift the weight forward. At the same time, the right hand stirs with the sword. The left Sword Fingers remain at the original position and intend to push back. Eyes look at the tip of the sword (Figure 2–42).

4. 重心繼續前移，右腳輕提向前上步成右弓步。同時，右手握劍繼續絞劍後前送，左手劍指經上向前

圖2–42

附於右前臂上，手心向下，眼看劍尖（圖2–43）。

(4) Continue to shift the weight forward. Lift the right foot gently and move it a step forward to form a Right Bow Step. Meanwhile, the right hand moves the sword forward after the stirring. The left Sword Fingers move forward to rest on the right forearm, palm facing down. Eyes look at the tip of the sword (Figure 2–43).

【要領】

（1）絞劍上步要輕靈、平穩，協調一致，不可忽高忽低。上步絞劍共三步，方向與壓劍方向一致。

（2）絞劍時要墜肘、旋腕，兩臂對拉；上步動作要連續，不可停頓；劍尖的運轉呈現螺旋形向前，

圖2–43

劍尖畫圓勿大。

【攻防含義】

若對方以劍向我腕部刺來，我手腕下沉避讓，隨即劍向右以劍尖刺對方腕部，一攻一防，形成絞劍動作。

Key Points

(1) The stirring and marching should be light, even, and coordinated with each other. Do not move up or down abruptly. The three steps are in the same direction as the last movement.

(2) When stirring with the sword, sink the elbow, turn the wrist and push the arms in the opposite directions. The forward steps should be continuous without pause. The tip of the sword is moving forward along a spiral track, the diameter of which should not be too large.

Application

If the opponent uses a sword to stab your wrist, sink your wrist to dodge it and then move the sword to the right to stab the opponent's wrist. The stirring is used for both offense and defense.

十六、提膝上刺

1. 上體略左轉，重心後移，左腿屈膝半蹲，右膝微屈。同時，右手握劍屈肘回抽帶至左腹前，手心向上，劍身平直，劍尖向右，左手劍指附於劍柄上，眼看劍尖方向（圖2-44）。

16. Thrust Upward and Raise Knee

(1) Turn the upper body to the left slightly. Shift the weight backward. Bend the left knee in a half squat. Bend the right knee slightly. Meanwhile, draw the sword back in front of the left abdomen by bending the right arm, blade flat, tip pointing to the right and palm facing up. Place the left Sword Fingers on the hilt of the sword. Eyes look at the tip of the sword (Figure 2–44).

2. 上體右轉，重心前移，右腿自然直立，左腿屈膝提起成右獨立步。同時，右手握劍向前上方刺出，手心向上，劍尖略高於頭，左手劍指附於右前臂內側，眼看劍尖（圖2–45）。

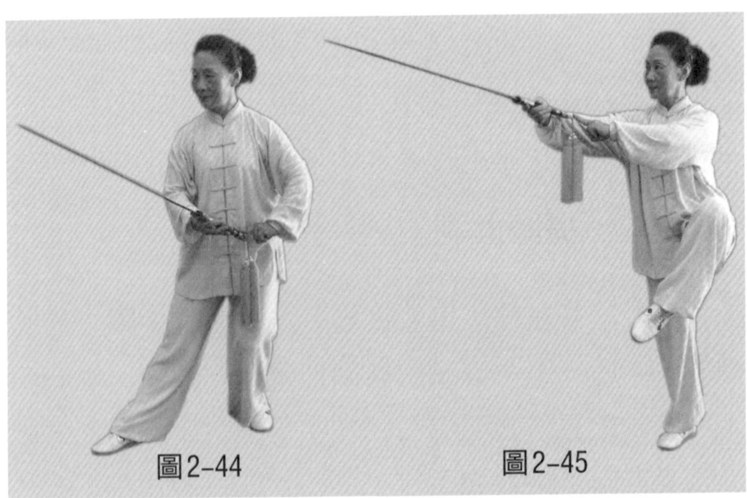

圖2–44 圖2–45

(2) Turn the upper body to the right. Shift the weight forward. The right leg stands straight naturally. Bend the left leg and lift it to form a Right One Leg Stand. At the same time, thrust the sword towards the upper front, palm facing up and the tip slightly higher than the head. The left Sword Fingers now touch the inside of the right forearm. Eyes look at the tip of the sword (Figure 2–45).

【要領】

(1) 絞劍後，先前送再回帶，轉腰提膝的同時上刺劍。轉腰、提膝、上刺要協調一致。

(2) 提膝不可低於腰，上體保持端正自然，不要前傾。劍尖略高於頭。

【攻防含義】

若對方以劍刺我胸部，我劍從右繞於對方劍上，貼其劍下壓回帶化開後，進身用劍刺擊對方頭部。

Key Points

(1) After stirring with the sword, send the sword forward first and then draw it back. At the same time, following the body turn, lift the knee, and thrust the sword to the upper front. The three movements should be coordinated with each other.

(2) The lifted knee should not be lower than the waist.

Keep the upper body upright naturally; do not lean forward. The tip of the sword is slightly higher than the head.

Application

If the opponent attacks your chest with a sword, move your sword over his sword, pressing it and pushing it aside. Then step forward and thrust your sword at your opponent's head.

十七、虛步下截

1. 右腿屈膝，身體下沉，左腳向左後落步，腳跟著地，上體左轉。同時，右手握劍隨轉體屈肘外旋向左上方帶劍，手心向上，腕同頭齊高，劍尖向右；左手劍指翻轉下落於左腰間，手心向上，眼向右看（圖2–46）。

17. Intercept Downward in Empty Step

(1) Bend the right knee and lower the body. The left foot takes a step to the left back, only the heel touching the ground. Turn the upper body to the left. Meanwhile, with the elbow bent, the right hand turn outward to draw the sword to the upper left, palm facing up, wrist at head level and the tip of the sword pointing to the right. Turn the left Sword Fingers over and place it at the left side of waist, palm facing up. Eyes look to the right (Figure 2–46).

2. 上體右轉，重心左移，左腳踏實並屈膝半蹲，右腳向左移半步，腳尖點地成右虛步。同時，右手握劍隨轉體略向左帶後向右下方截劍至右胯旁，劍尖向左前，與膝同高，勁貫劍身下刃；左手劍指翻轉畫弧上舉於頭左上方，手心斜向上，眼向右看（圖2-47）。

(2) Turn the upper body to the right. Shift the weight to the left. Place the left foot on the ground solidly and bend the knee in a half squat. The right foot takes a half step to the left, only the toes touching the ground to form a Right Empty Step. Meanwhile, the right hand follows the body, first moving the sword to the left slightly, then intercepting to the lower right. Stop at the right side of the hip, the tip of the sword pointing

圖2-46　圖2-47

left front at knee level. Deliver the force to the lower edge. The left Sword Fingers turn over and draw an arc to the upper left of the head, palm facing diagonally up. Eyes look to the right (Figure 2-47).

【要領】

（1）下截劍時，要以腰向右轉動帶動右臂向右下方截按，身、劍、手、腳、眼動作要協調一致，同時到位；右臂微屈，不可挺直；劍身與身體平行。

（2）右虛步要偏左30°，眼要向右前方看，右腳尖方向與視角方向夾角約90°。

（3）兩腳橫向距離在10公分左右，不可交叉或過寬。

【攻防含義】

若對方以劍向我右腿刺來，我右腳向左上閃開後，隨即用劍截擊對方腕部或刺劍。

Key Points

(1) When intercepting downward, turn the waist to the right leading the sword to cut toward the lower right. The motions of the body, sword, hands, feet and eyes are coordinated with each other and finished at the same time. Bend the right arm slightly; do not be stiff. The blade of the sword is parallel to the body.

(2) The Right Empty Step points 30° to the left from the centre of the body. Eyes look to the right front 90° from the direction of the right foot.

(3) The horizontal distance of the feet is about 10 cm; the feet should not be crossed or too far apart.

Application

If the opponent attacks your right leg, move your right foot to the upper left to dodge, and then intercept or stab his wrist with your sword.

十八、右左平帶

1. 左膝微屈，右腿屈膝提起，腳尖下垂。同時，右手握劍立刃向前伸送，與胸同高，臂自然伸直，劍尖略低於手，左手劍指經上向前附於右前臂內側，眼看劍尖（圖2-48）。

18. Withdraw Sword-Right and Left

(1) Bend the left knee slightly. Bend the right leg and lift the knee up, the toes hanging down. In the meantime, stretch the right arm naturally straight, moving the sword to the front with its blade vertical at the chest level. The tip of the sword is slightly lower than the hand. The left Sword Fingers move forward to the inside of the right forearm. Eyes look at the tip of the sword(Figure 2-48).

2. 右腳向右前方落步，上體略右轉成右弓步。同時，右手握劍前伸，手心翻轉向下後屈肘向右帶至右肋前，劍尖朝前對準身體中線，左手仍處於右前臂內側，眼看劍尖（圖2–49）。

(2) The right foot takes a step to the right front. Turn the upper body to form a Right Bow Step. Meanwhile, after holding

圖2–48
圖2–49

the sword forward, right hand turn over to make the palm face down and withdraw the sword to the front of the right ribs by bending the elbow, the tip pointing forward to the centre of the body. The left Sword Fingers remain on the inside of the right forearm. Eyes look at the tip of the sword (Figure 2–49).

3. 重心移至右腳，左腳收至右腳內側再向左前方上步，重心再移向左腳，成左弓步。同時，右手握劍隨劍尖前伸，前臂外旋翻轉手心向上後微屈肘向左肋前平帶，劍尖向前對準身體中線；左手劍指經下向左，臂呈弧形舉於頭左上方，手心斜向上，眼看前方（圖2–50）。

(3) Shift the weight onto the right foot. The left foot first

圖2–50

moves to the inside of the right foot then takes a step to the left front, and shift the weight onto the left foot to form a Left Bow Step. At the same time, the right hand moves the sword forward with the tip ahead. Then turn over the forearm to make the palm face up. Withdraw the sword to the front of left ribs, the tip aligning with the centre of the body. The left hand draw an arc upward to the upper left of the head, palm facing up. Eyes look ahead (Figure 2–50).

【要領】

（1）弓步與帶劍協調一致；不可前俯上體或突臀。

（2）左右帶劍時要有前伸再帶之意，劍尖走橢圓，劍尖始終對正前方，不可外展。

【攻防含義】

若對方以劍刺我右胸，我劍前伸貼其劍向右後平帶化開。若對方以劍刺我左胸，我劍前伸貼其劍，上步向左後平帶化開。

Key Points

(1) The Bow Step and withdrawing the sword should be coordinated with each other. Do not bend forward or push out the buttocks.

(2) When withdrawing the sword to the left or right, the

tip is moved in an ellipse by moving the sword forward first and then withdrawing it backward. The tip points to the front at all times.

Application

If the opponent attacks your right chest with a sword, you can move your sword forward to meet the coming sword and lead it away to the right. If the opponent attacks your left chest, you just step forward, thrusting out your sword to meet the sword and lead it away to the left.

十九、弓步劈劍

1. 隨重心前移，右腳擺步向前，屈膝半蹲；左腿自然伸直，腳跟提起，上體右轉。同時，右手握劍向右後下方後截，左手劍指屈肘弧形向下落於右肩前，手心斜向後下方，眼看劍尖（圖2-51）。

19. Chop in Bow Step

(1) When shifting the weight forward, the right foot steps forward in a Toes Out Step. Bend the knee in a half squat. Extend the left leg naturally straight and lift the heel. Turn the upper body to the right. Meanwhile, the right hand holds the sword to intercept to the lower back. Bend the left elbow and move the left Sword Fingers in an arc to the right shoulder, palm facing diagonally to the lower back. Eyes look at the tip of

the sword (Figure 2–51).

2. 上體左轉，左腳向前上步屈膝成左弓步。同時，右手握劍經上向前掄劈，高與肩平，劍身與臂成一直線；左手劍指經下向左上畫弧，臂呈弧形舉於頭左上方，手心斜向上，眼看前方（圖2–52）。

(2) Turn the upper body to the left. Move the left foot for–

圖2–51
圖2–52

ward and bend the knee to form a Left Bow Step. Meanwhile, the right hand holds the sword to make a Swing Chop forward, with the tip at shoulder level and the blade aligning with the arm. The left Sword Fingers move in an arc to the upper left of the head, arm arched and palm facing diagonally up. Eyes look ahead (Figure 2–52).

【要領】

（1）叉步下截時，上步要大，擰腰，上體稍前傾，眼向後看劍尖。

（2）弓步劈劍時，右手劍先外旋翻，再上弓步掄劈。

（3）上右步與回身截劍；左弓步與掄劈劍要協調一致，動作連貫自然。

【攻防含義】

若對方以劍向我右前刺來，我則上左弓步閃身，用劍向對方頭部掄劈。

Key Points

(1) While cutting down in Backward Crossover Step, take a big step. Twist the waist. Lean the upper body forward slightly. Eyes look back at the tip of the sword.

(2) When chopping down in Bow Step, turn the right hand outward first then step forward with the left foot and chop

downward.

(3) The right foot stepping forward and turning the body to intercept with the sword are coordinated with each other. The same applies to the Left Bow Step and the swing. The movement should be continuous and natural.

Application

If the opponent thrusts sword towards your right front, take the left Bow Step to dodge it and then swing the sword to chop down towards the opponent's head.

二十、丁步托劍

1. 隨重心前移，右腿屈膝上提成獨立步。同時，上體右轉並微微前傾，右手握劍隨轉體向右後方截劍，左手劍指屈肘擺至右肩前，手心向右後，眼看劍尖（圖2–53）。

20. Lift Sword in T–Step

(1) Shift the weight forward. Lift the right knee to form a One Leg Stand. At the same time, turn the upper body to the right and lean forward slightly. Intercept towards the right back with the sword. Move the left Sword Fingers to the right shoulder, palm facing to the right back. Eyes look at the tip of the sword (Figure 2–53).

2. 右腳向前落步，屈膝半蹲，左腳跟步至右腳內側，腳尖點地成左丁步。同時，右手握劍向前，屈肘向上托劍，劍尖向右；左手劍指附於右腕內側，手心向外，眼看右側（圖2-54）。

（2）The right foot steps forward. Bend the right knee in a half squat. The left foot follows up to the inside of the right foot, with only the toes touching the ground to form a Left T-shape Step. Meanwhile, move the right hand forward and bend the elbow to lift the sword, the tip pointing right. The left Sword Fingers touch to the inside of the right wrist, palm facing outward. Eyes look to the right (Figure 2-54).

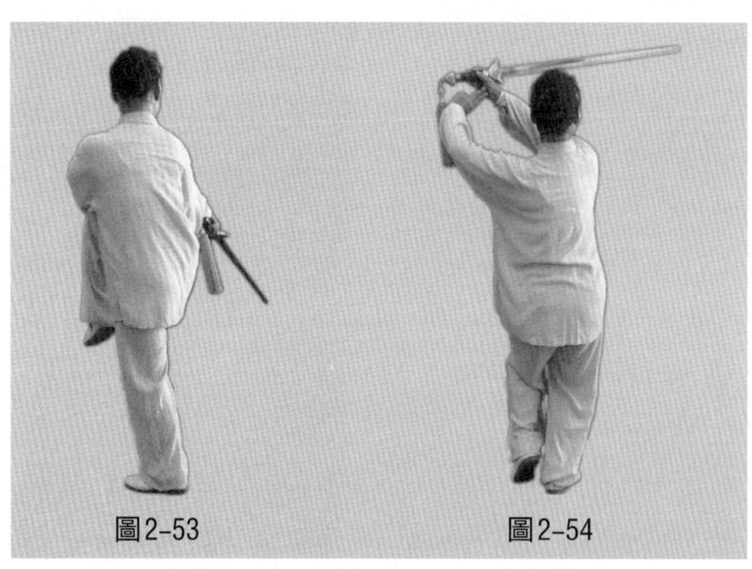
圖2-53 圖2-54

【要領】

（1）提膝與回身下截劍，丁步與托劍要協調一致。

（2）劍上托時，兩手置於頭左側，劍身不要遮住眼睛，勁貫劍身上刃。

（3）上體正直，不可蹋腰凸臀，整個動作要柔和連貫。

【攻防含義】

若對方以劍劈我頭部，我急上步進身避開，並橫劍由下向上，以劍身後部小指側劍刃托架其臂或腕。

Key Points

(1) Lifting the knee and turning body to cut down are co-ordinated. The same applies to the T-shape Step and lifting the sword.

(2) When lifting sword up, both hands are at the left side of the head in order for the blade not to block the sight. Deliver the force to the upper edge of the sword.

(3) Keep the upper body upright. Do not bend the waist or push out the buttocks. The whole movement should be gentle and continuous.

Application

If the opponent cleaves toward your head with a sword, you can quickly step forward to avoid it and then raise the sword to lift his arm or wrist.

二十一、分腳後點

1. 左腳向左前方上步，腳尖內扣，膝微屈，上體右轉約90°；隨以右腳前掌為軸，腳跟內轉，膝微屈。右手握劍向右向下畫弧至腕與肩同高，手心斜朝上，劍尖斜向下，左手劍指仍附於右腕，眼看劍尖（圖2-55）。

21. Separate Foot and Point Sword Back

(1) The left foot takes a step to the left front. Swing the left toes inward and bend the knee slightly. Turn the upper body 90° to the right. Pivoting on the right forefoot, turn the heel inward and bend the knee slightly. The right hand moves

圖2-55

the sword to the right then downward in an arc until the wrist is at shoulder level, palm facing diagonally up and the tip of the sword pointing diagonally down. The left Sword Fingers stay on the right wrist. Eyes look at the tip of the sword (Figure 2–55).

2. 右腳向後撤步，腿自然伸直；左腳以腳跟為軸，腳尖內扣碾步，屈膝半蹲，上體右轉約90°。同時，右手握劍，劍尖領先，經下向後畫弧穿至腹前，手心向外，劍尖向右，稍低於腕，左手劍指仍附於腕，眼看劍尖方向（圖2–56）。

(2) The right foot steps backward. Extend the right leg naturally straight. Pivot on the left heel to turn the toes inward

圖2–56

and bend the knee in a half squat. Turn the upper body 90° to the right. Meanwhile, the right hand draws the sword in an arc downward first then backward and stops in front of the abdomen, palm facing outward, the tip of the sword pointing right and slightly lower than the wrist. The left Sword Fingers stay on the right wrist. Eyes look at the tip of the sword (Figure 2–56).

3. 隨重心前移，右腿屈膝前弓成右弓步，上體略右轉。同時，右手握劍沿右腿內側向前穿刺，與肩同高；左手劍指向左後方畫弧擺舉，與肩同高，手心向外，眼看劍尖（圖2–57）。

(3) While shifting the weight forward, bend the right leg

圖2–57

to form a Right Bow Step. Turn the upper body to the right slightly. Meanwhile, move the sword along the inside of the right leg and thrust it forward to the shoulder height. The left Sword Fingers swing to the left back and draw an arc to the level of shoulder, palm facing outward. Eyes look at the tip of the sword (Figure 2–57).

4. 隨重心前移，左腳向右腳併步，兩腿屈膝半蹲，上體略右轉。劍柄領先，向上向左畫弧帶劍至左胯旁，手心向內，劍尖朝左上方；左手劍指向上擺與右手相合後，屈肘下落附於右腕內側，眼看左側（圖2–58）。

(4) Continue to shift the weight forward. Place the left foot together with the right foot. Bend the legs in a half squat and turn the upper body to the right slightly. With the hilt ahead, move the sword upward and leftward to draw an arc to the left side of the hip, palm facing inward and the tip pointing to the upper left. The left Sword Fingers swing upward to meet the right hand and fall down to the inside of the right wrist by bending the elbow. Eyes look to the left (Figure 2–58).

5. 身體上升，左腿自然伸直，右腿屈膝提起，腳尖自然下垂，上體右轉約90°。同時，右手握劍使劍尖在上體左側立圓畫弧至後下方時，以劍柄領先，前臂內旋上提舉至頭前上方，手心向右，劍尖向前下方；左手劍指外旋，向前下方伸出到右腳踝內側前方，手心向前上方，眼看前方（圖2-59）。

(5) Raise the body. Extend the left leg naturally straight. Bend the right leg and lift it up, the toes naturally hanging down. Turn the upper body about 90° to the right. Meanwhile, the right hand holds the sword and draws a vertical arc with the tip at the left side of the upper body. when the tip get the lower back, with the hilt ahead, turn the forearm inward to lift the sword to the upper front of the head, palm facing right and the tip pointing the lower front. Turn the left Sword Fingers outward and place it at the inside of the right ankle, the palm facing

圖2-58 圖2-59

the upper front. Eyes look ahead (Figure 2–59).

6. 右腳向前擺踢成分腳。同時，上體略向右擰轉，隨轉體右手握劍經上向右後方提腕點劍，腕同肩平；左手劍指向左上方擺舉，臂呈弧形，手舉於頭左上方，手心斜向上，眼看劍尖（圖2–60）。

(6) Lift the right foot up and kick it out to form Separating Feet. At the same time, twist the upper body to the right slightly. Move the right hand to the right back and lift the wrist to point the sword down, wrist at shoulder level. The left Sword Fingers swing to the upper left of the head, arm arched and palm facing diagonally up. Eyes look at the tip of the sword (Figure 2–60).

圖2–60

【要領】

（1）提膝與提劍、分腳與後點劍要協調一致，連貫圓活，一氣呵成。

（2）分腳點劍，上體要正直，不要後仰。

（3）提劍時與劍指向前下伸穿要對拔，以保持身體平穩。

【攻防含義】

若對方以劍從後方刺來，我向側後揮劍點擊對方頭部。

Key Points

(1) Lifting the knee and lifting the sword, separating the feet and pointing the sword down should be coordinated with each other. The movement should be continuous and smooth and finished as a whole.

(2) While separating the feet and pointing the sword down, keep the upper body upright. Do not bend backward.

(3) When pulling the sword up and extending the Sword Fingers to the lower front, push both hands in the opposite directions in order to keep the body stable.

Application

If the opponent uses a sword to thrust from your back, you can wield the sword backward to stab at his head.

第三組

二十二、仆步穿劍（右）

1. 左腿屈膝半蹲，右腿屈膝向後落步，成左弓步。同時，上體左轉，隨轉體右手握劍弧形向體前擺舉，腕同胸高，手心向上，劍身平直，劍尖向前；左手劍指向下，屈肘附於右前臂內側，手心向下，眼看劍尖（圖2-61）。

Group 3

22. Thrust Sword in Crouch Step－Right

(1) Bend the left leg in a half squat. Lift the right leg and step backward to form a Left Bow Step. At the same time, turn

圖2-61

the upper body to the left. The right hand holds the sword and draws an arc in front of the chest, wrist at chest level, palm facing up. The blade of the sword is flat, tip pointing forward. Move the left Sword Fingers down to the inside of right forearm, palm facing downward. Eyes look at the tip of the sword (Figure 2–61).

2. 隨身體重心後移，兩腳以腳掌為軸碾步，身體右轉約90°成右橫弓步。同時，右手握劍屈肘經胸前向右擺舉斬劍，臂微屈，手心朝上，劍尖略高於腕；左手劍指向左分展側舉，與腰齊平，臂微屈，手心向外，眼看劍尖（圖2–62）。

(2) Shift the weight backward. Pivoting on both forefeet,

圖2–62

turn the body 90° to the right to form a Right Bow Step. At the same time, the right hand holds the sword, passing in front of the chest. Cut to the right, the arm bent slightly and palm facing up. The tip of the sword is a little higher than the wrist. Move the left Sword Fingers to the left side of the body, at waist level, the arm bent slightly, palm facing outward. Eyes look at the tip of the sword (Figure 2-62).

3. 重心左移，成左橫弓步，上體略左轉。同時，右手握劍屈臂上舉，帶至頭前偏左上方，手心向內，劍身平直，劍尖朝右；左手劍指向上擺舉，附於右腕內側，臂呈弧形，手心向外，眼看劍尖方向（圖2-63）。

(3) Shift the weight to the left. Form a right Bow Step. Turn the upper body to the left. At the same time, the right hand holds the sword and rises above the left side of the forehead, palm facing inward. The tip of the sword is pointing right and a little higher than the wrist, the blade flat. Move the left Sword Fingers upward and rest them on the inside of the right wrist, arm arched and palm facing outward. Eyes look at the tip of the sword (Figure 2-63).

4. 左腿屈膝全蹲成右仆步，上體略右轉。同時，右手握劍向下置於襠前，手心向外，使劍立劍落至右腿內側，劍尖向右，左手劍指仍附於右腕，眼看劍尖方向（圖2-64）。

(4) Bend the left knee in a squat and form a Crouch Step. Shift the weight to the right slightly. At the same time, the right hand holds the sword and places it in front of the crotch, palm facing outward. The edge of the sword is up, tip pointing right. Place the left Sword Fingers on the right wrist. Eyes look at the tip of the sword (Figure 2-64).

5. 隨重心右移，右腳尖外展，左腳尖內扣碾步成右弓步。同時，身體右轉約90°，隨轉體右手握劍沿右腿內側向前立劍穿出，腕與胸同高，臂自然伸直，手

圖2-64
圖2-63

心向左，左手劍指仍附於右腕內側，眼看前方（圖2-65）。

（5）Shifting the weight to the right, swing the right toes outward, the left toes inward to form a Right Bow Step. Meanwhile, turn the body 90° to the right. The right hand follows the body to thrust the sword forward along the inside of the right thigh, with the sword upright, wrist at chest level, arm extended naturally, palm facing left. Place the left Sword Fingers on the inside of the right wrist. Eyes look at the tip of the sword (Figure 2-65).

【要領】

（1）身體重心左右轉換要保持平穩，上體不可

圖2-65

搖晃。仆步穿劍時，不可彎腰低頭。

（2）動作時，以身帶臂，使劍動作連貫圓活。

（3）中老年者在做仆步時如有困難，可姿勢高一點成半蹲仆步。

【攻防含義】

若對方以劍刺我胸，我向左閃身，同時以劍貼著對方劍向左帶化，接著右仆步劍下落，閃開對方來劍後，立即重心前移接近對方，以劍刺對方胸部。

Key Points

(1) When shifting the weight to the left or right, keep the body steady; do not sway. When thrusting the sword, do not bend the waist or bow the head.

(2) Use waist to lead the arm, moving smoothly.

(3) If it is too difficult to do a full Crouch Step, make a half Crouch Step instead.

Application

If an opponent stab at your chest with a sword, move to the left and push his sword to the left, then lower your sword with a Crouch Step. After dodging the attack, shift the weight close to the opponent and thrust your sword at his chest.

二十三、蹬腳架劍（左）

1. 右腳尖外展，身體略右轉。同時，右手持劍向右上方帶劍至頭前右上方，腕距頭約10公分，手心向外，劍尖向前；左手劍指屈肘附於右前臂內側，手心向外，眼看劍尖方向（圖2–66）。

23. Lift Sword and Kick with the Left Heel

(1) Swinging the right toes outward, turn the body to the right slightly. At the same time, the right hand holds the sword, moves to the upper right, and stops at the right side of the fore–head, the wrist is 10cm from the head, palm facing, the tip of the sword pointing forward. Bend the left elbow and rest the left Sword Fingers on the inside of the right forearm, palm facing outward. Eyes look at the tip of the sword (Figure 2–66).

2. 右腿自然直立，左腳經右腳踝內側屈膝提起，

圖2–66

腳尖自然下垂。同時，右手握劍略向右帶，眼看劍尖方向（圖2–67）。

(2) The right leg stands straight. Lift the left foot passing the inside of the right foot, the toes stretching down. At the same time, the right hand holds the sword and moves to the right slightly. Eyes look at the tip of the sword (Figure 2–67).

3. 左腳以腳跟為力點向左側蹬腳。同時，右手握劍上架，臂微屈；左手劍指向左側前指，臂自然伸直，腕同肩平，手心向前，指尖向上，眼看劍尖方向（圖2–68）。

(3) The left foot kicks to the left with the force on the heel. At the same time, the right hand holds the sword and parry

圖2–67　圖2–68

over the head; the arm is bent. The left Sword Fingers point to the left front, extend the arm naturally, the wrist at should lev–el, palm facing forward, fingertips pointing up. Eyes look at the tip of the sword (Figure 2–68).

【要領】

（1）定勢時，劍指、劍尖、蹬腳方向一致。

（2）蹬腳與架劍、劍指三個動作要協調一致。

（3）右腳獨立要站穩，架劍時右手要上撐，氣向下沉，以助平衡。

（4）蹬腳時，腳不可低於腰，腳尖要回勾。

【攻防含義】

若對方以劍刺或劈我頭部，我向右轉身，同時以劍貼著對方劍向右向上帶架化開，以左腳蹬對方腹部或胸部。

Key Points

(1) When the movement is complete, the Sword Figures and Tip of the sword are in the same direction as the kick.

(2) The Sword Figures are coordinated with the lifting the sword and kicking.

(3) Stand on the right foot steadily. Push the right hand upward to lift the sword. Sink the energy to gain the balance.

(4) When kicking, the foot is no lower than the waist.

The toes point to the back.

Application

If an opponent thrust his sword to your head, turn your body to the right and push his sword to the right and upward then kick his abdomen or chest.

二十四、提膝點劍（左）

左腿屈膝成右獨立步，上體略右轉。同時，右手握劍經上向右前下方點劍，劍尖與膝同高；左手劍指屈肘右擺，附於右前臂內側，手心向下，眼看劍尖方向（圖2-69）。

【要領】

（1）左腿屈膝與點劍要協調一致。

圖2-69

（2）右腿獨立站穩，左膝要高於腰，腳面展平並向內護襠。

【攻防含義】

若對方從右側俯身以劍擊我右腿，我則揮劍由上向右前點擊對方頭或腕。

24. Point Sword Down and Lift the Left Knee

Bend the left leg and stand on the right leg. Turn the body to the right slightly. At the same time, the right hand holds the sword and points it down to the lower front, tip at knee level. Bend the left elbow and place the left Sword Fingers on the inside of the right forearm, palm facing down. Eyes look at the tip of the sword (Figure 2–69).

Key Points

(1) Bend the left knee in coordination with pointing the sword.

(2) Stand on the right foot steady. The foot is no lower than the waist, toes pointing inward to protect the crotch.

Application

If an opponent thrusts his sword to your right leg from the right, wield your sword to the right front to stab his head or wrist.

二十五、仆步橫掃（左）

1. 右腿屈膝全蹲，左腳向左後方落步成左仆步，上體略左轉。同時，左手劍指屈肘內旋，從左肋前向後反插至左腿外側，手心向外；右手握劍沉腕下落至右膝前上方，手心翻轉向上，眼看劍尖（圖2-70）。

25. Swing Sword in Crouch Step-Left

(1) Bend the right leg in a squat. Lift the left foot and step backward to form a left Crouch Step. Turn the upper body to the left. At the same time, bend the left elbow and rotate it inward, then move it along the outside of the left leg, palm facing outward. The right hand holds sword and wrist sinks in right front of the right knee, palm turning over to face up. Eyes look at the tip of the sword (Figure 2-70).

2. 隨身體重心左移，上體左轉約90°，左腿屈膝，

圖2-70

腳尖外展，右腳跟外展碾步成左弓步。同時，右手握劍向左平掃，腕同腰平，手心向上，臂微屈，劍尖向前下方，略低於腕；左手劍指經左向上，臂呈弧形舉於頭左上方，手心斜向上，眼看劍尖（圖2-71）。

(2) As the weight is shifting to the left, turn the upper body to the left 90° . Bend the left leg and swing the toes outward. Pivot on the right heel to form a left Bow Step. At the same time, the right hand holds the sword and sweeps to the left, wrist at waist level, palm facing up, arm bent slightly. The tip of the sword is pointing to the lower front and a little lower than the wrist. Move the left Sword Fingers upward from the left side of the body and stop above the left side of the head, the arm arched, palm facing upward diagonally. Eyes

圖2-71

look at the tip of the sword (Figure 2–71).

【要領】

（1）做仆步時，中老年者可為高仆步。仆步轉換為弓步時上體不要前傾和凸臀。

（2）掃劍時要以腰帶臂，勁達劍刃，劍柄稍先於劍尖。

【攻防含義】

若對方以劍擊我頭，我以仆步下勢閃開，並進身以劍橫掃對方腿部。

Key Points

(1) If it is too difficult to do a full Crouch Step, make a half Crouch Step instead. When moving from the Crouch Step to a Bow Step, do not bend forward or push the buttocks out.

(2) Use waist to lead the arm, deliver the force to the edge, the handle ahead the tip.

Application

If an opponent attack your head with a sword, dodge it in the Crouch Step and move close to the opponent and sweep his legs with your sword.

二十六、弓步下截（右、左）

1. 重心前移，右腳收至左腳內側，腳不點地。同時，右手握劍內旋畫弧撥劍，腕同腰高，手心向下，劍尖向左前下方；左手劍指屈肘下落於右腕內側，手心向下，眼看劍尖（圖2-72）。

26. Intercept Downward in Bow Step (Right and Left)

(1) Shift the weight forward. Bring the right foot and place it beside the left foot without touching the ground. At the same time, the right hand holds the sword and rotates inward, wrist at waist level, palm facing down, and the tip of the sword pointing lower front. Bend the left elbow and move the left Sword Fingers down to the inside of the right wrist, palm facing downward. Eyes look at the tip of the sword (Figure 2-72).

2. 右腳向右前方上步成右弓步，上體略右轉。同時，右手握劍向右前方畫弧截劍，臂微屈，腕同胸高，虎口向下，劍尖朝前下方，左手劍指仍附於右腕，眼看劍尖（圖2-73）。

(2) The right foot steps to the right front to form a Right Bow Step. Turn the upper body to the right slightly. At the same time, the right hand holds the sword and intercepts to the right front in an arc, the arm bent slightly, wrist at chest level, the Tiger Mouth facing down. The tip of the sword is facing downward. Place the left Sword Fingers on the right wrist. Eyes look at the tip of the sword (Figure 2-73).

3. 上體重心移至右腿，左腳跟收至右腳內側，腳不觸地，上體右轉。同時，右手握劍外旋畫弧撥劍至右胯旁，手心向上，劍尖向右前下方；左手劍指附於右腕內側，手心向下，眼看劍尖（圖2-74）。

(3) Shift the weight onto the right leg. Bring the left foot and place it beside the right foot, without touching the ground. Turn the upper body to the right. At the same time, the right hand holds the sword and pulls it in an arc to the right hip, palm facing up, and the tip of the sword pointing lower right front. Place the left Sword Fingers on the inside of right wrist, palm facing downward. Eyes look at the tip of the sword (Figure 2-74).

圖2-72　圖2-73

4. 左腳向左前方上步，身體重心左移，右腳跟外展成左弓步，上體左轉約45°。同時，右手握劍向左畫弧截劍至身體左前方，臂微屈，腕同胸高，手心向上，劍尖朝前下方；左手劍指向左前上方畫弧擺舉，臂呈弧形舉於頭前左上方，手心斜向上，眼看劍尖（圖2-75）。

(4) The left foot steps to the left front. Shift the weight to the left and swing the right toes outward to form a Left Bow Step. Turn the upper body 45° to the left. At the same time, the right hand holds the sword and intercepts to the left front in an arc, the arm bent slightly, wrist at chest level, and palm facing

圖2-74 圖2-75

up. The tip of the sword is facing lower front. The left Sword Fingers draw an arc to the upper left front, bending the elbow above the left side of the forehead, palm facing up diagonally. Eyes look at the tip of the sword (Figure 2–75).

【要領】

（1）收腳撥劍時要鬆胯斂臀，不要塌腰凸臀；撥劍要以腕為軸，劍尖形成一小圓弧。

（2）弓步截劍時要鬆腰沉胯，上體正直，不要前俯；截劍要以身帶劍，身隨步轉。

（3）整個動作要柔和連貫，眼隨劍走。

【攻防含義】

若對方以劍刺我腹部，我右手握劍提腕，以劍身貼對方來劍向左（右）畫弧撥開，然後進身以劍截擊對方下盤。

Key Points

(1) When bringing in the foot and pulling the sword, relax the hips; pull the buttocks in; do not bend the waist or push the buttocks out. Use the wrist as an axle to pull the sword, the tip drawing a small arc.

(2) When intercepting in the Bow Step, relax the waist; sink the hip. Keep the upper body upright; do not bend forward. Body leads the sword, the body follows the step.

(3) Complete the movement continuously and smoothly.

Application

If an opponent thrusts his sword at your abdomen, move your sword towards his and push it away, then step forward to intercept his lower body.

二十七、弓步下刺

1. 重心前移，右腳在左腳後震腳，屈膝半蹲，左腳跟提起，上體略右轉。同時，右手握劍屈肘回帶至右肋前，手心向上，劍尖朝前，略低於手；左手劍指先前伸，復隨右手回帶屈肘附於右腕內側，手心朝下，眼看劍尖（圖2-76）。

27. Thrust Sword Down in Bow Step

(1) Shift the weight forward. The right foot makes a Stamp Step behind the left foot. Bend the right knee in a half squat. Lift the left heel off the ground. At the same time, the right hand holds the sword and moves it to the right ribs, palm facing up. The tip of the sword is pointing forward and is lower than the hand. The left Sword Fingers move forward and follow the right hand, the arm is bent, palm facing downward. Place the left Sword Fingers on the inside of right wrist. Eyes look at the tip of the sword (Figure 2-76).

2. 左腳向左前方上步，重心前移成左弓步，上體略左轉。同時，右手握劍向左前下方刺出，腕同腰平，手心向上；左手劍指仍附於右腕內側，手心向下，眼看劍尖（圖2–77）。

(2) The left foot steps to the left front and shift the weight forward to form a Left Bow Step. Turn the upper body to the left slightly. At the same time, the right hand holds the sword and thrust it to the lower left front, wrist at chest level, palm facing up. Place the left Sword Fingers on the inside of right wrist, palm facing down. Eyes look at the tip of the sword (Figure 2–77).

圖2–76　圖2–77

【要領】

（1）震腳與刺劍均為發力動作。震腳與兩手相合屈肘回帶，刺劍與弓步均要協調一致。

（2）震腳時，要全腳垂直下踏，不要向後跳躍。右腳跟震地面的同時掀起左腳跟，不可跳起。

（3）刺劍時，先轉腰回帶為之蓄勁，繼而以轉腰沉胯順劍下刺，力注劍尖，發勁要鬆彈。刺劍方向在左前方約30°。

Key Points

(1) Stamp and Thrust forcefully. The stamp and the hands holding together are coordinated. The same applies to the thrust and the Bow Step.

(2) When stamping, the entire foot falls down vertically; do not jump backward. As the foot falls on the ground, the other's heel is off the ground; do not jump to the air.

(3) When thrusting, turn the waist to gather the power, then turn the waist back and sink the hip to thrust the sword down to 30° to the left front. Deliver the force to the tip of the sword. Release the power elastically.

二十八、右左雲抹

1. 隨身體重心前移，右腳跟進左腳內側，腳不觸地，身體略左轉。同時，右手握劍沉腕略向左帶，腕與胸平，臂微屈，手心向上，劍尖略低於手；左手劍指略向左帶後經胸前向右畫弧至右臂上方，手心向外，眼看劍尖（圖2-78）。

28. Cloud and Slide – Right and Left

(1) Shift the weight forward. The right foot follows up beside the left foot without touching the ground. Turn the upper body to the left slightly. At the same time, the right hand holds the sword. Sink the right wrist and draw the sword back to the left, wrist at chest level, arm bent and palm facing up. The tip of the sword is a little lower than the hand. Move the left Sword Fingers to the left first, then past in front of the chest to the right and stop above the right arm, palm facing outward. Eyes

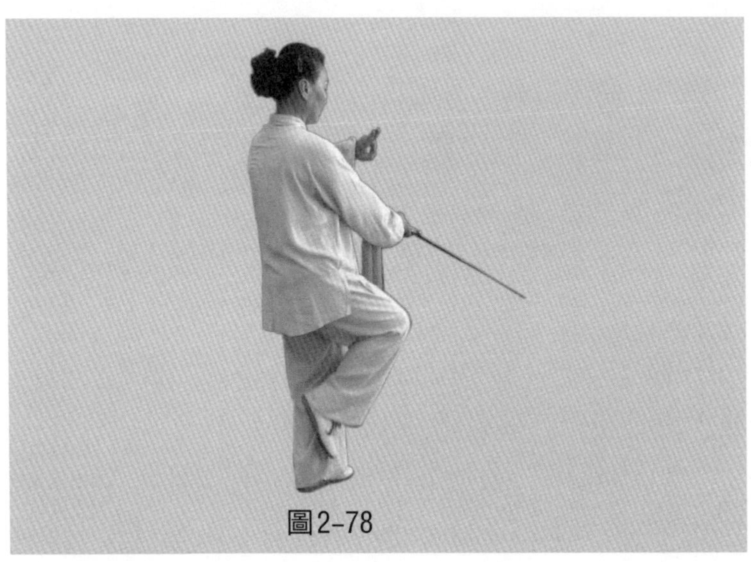
圖2-78

look at the tip of the sword (Figure 2-78).

2. 右腳向右略前上步成右橫弓步，上體右轉。同時，右手握劍向右上方畫弧削劍，臂微屈；左手劍指向左畫弧分展舉於左前方，與胸平，手心向外，眼看劍尖（圖2-79）。

(2) The right foot steps to the right front to form a right Side Bow Step. Turn the upper body to the right. At the same time, the right hand holds the sword and peels upward in an arc, arm bent slightly. Move the left Sword Fingers to the left and extend the arm at the left front of the body at chest level, palm facing outward. Eyes look at the tip of the sword (Figure 2-79).

3. 上體略右轉，身體重心右移，繼而上體略左轉，左腳向右蓋步，膝微屈；右腳在左腳即將落地時，蹬地屈膝後舉於左小腿後，腳尖下垂，離地約10公分。同時，右手握劍在面前隨上體旋轉逆時針畫弧雲劍，擺至體前，手心翻轉向下，腕與胸平，臂微屈，劍尖向左前方；左手劍指與右手在胸前相合，附於右腕內側，手心向下，眼看劍尖（圖2-80）。

(3) Turn the upper body to the right slightly. Shift the weight to the right. Then turn the upper body to the left slightly.

The left foot steps to the right to form a right Crossover Step, knee bent slightly. As the left foot touching the ground, the right foot pushes the ground. Bend the right leg and lift the foot backward behind the left lower leg, toes pointing down 10cm from the ground. At the same time, the right hand holds the sword and follows the body to draw an anticlockwise arc. The right hand stops in front of the body, wrist at chest level, arm bent and palm facing down. The tip of the sword is pointing to the left front. Move the left Sword Fingers in front of the body and place it on the inside of the right wrist, palm facing down. Eyes look at the tip of the sword(Figure 2–80).

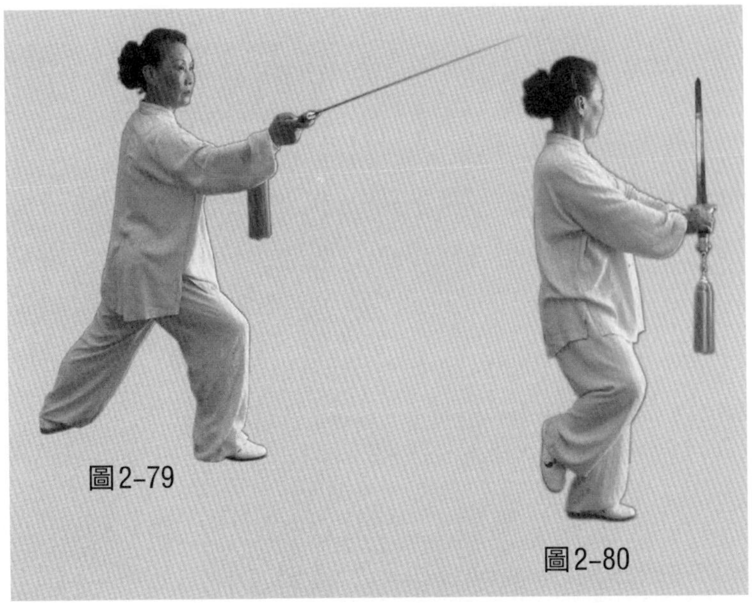
圖2–79

圖2–80

4. 右腳向左（右）偏前上步成右弓步，上體右轉。同時，右手握劍向右平抹至右前方，手心向下，左手劍指仍附於右腕內側，眼看劍尖方向（圖2–81）。

(4) The right foot steps to the left front to form a Right Bow Step. Turn the upper body to the right. At the same time, the right hand holds the sword and slides to the right front, palm facing down. The left Sword Fingers stay on the inside of the right wrist. Eyes look at the tip of the sword (Figure 2–81).

5. 身體重心移向右腳，左腳跟至右腳內側不觸地，上體略右轉。同時，右手握劍略屈肘右帶，高與腰平，劍尖向前，左手劍指仍附於右腕內側，眼看劍尖方向（圖2–82）。

(5) Shift the weight onto the right foot. The left foot follows up beside the right foot without touching the ground. Turn the upper body to the right slightly. At the same time, the right hand holds the sword and draws the sword back to the right, wrist at waist level, arm bent. The tip of the sword is pointing forward. The left Sword Fingers stays on the inside of the right wrist. Eyes look at the tip of the sword (Figure 2–82).

6. 左腳向左偏前上步成左弓步，上體左轉。同時，右手握劍向前伸送後向左抹帶，腕與胸平，手心向下，劍尖向前；左手劍指經前向左畫弧擺舉至身體左側，手心向外，眼看劍尖（圖2-83）。

(6) The left foot steps to the left front to form a Left Bow Step. Turn the upper body to the left. At the same time, the

圖2-81
圖2-82
圖2-83

right hand holds the sword and extends to slide to the left, wrist at chest level, palm facing down and the tip of the sword pointing forward. Move the left Sword Fingers to the left and stop at the left side of the body, palm facing outward. Eyes look at the tip of the sword (Figure 2–83).

7. 上體重心向左移動，右腳向左蓋步；右腳將落地時，左腳蹬地屈膝後舉於右小腿後，腳尖下垂，離地約10公分，上體略右轉。同時，右手握劍在面前順時針畫圓雲劍，擺至體前，與胸齊平，手心向上，劍尖向右前方；左手劍指在雲劍時向右與右手相合，附於右腕內側，手心向下，眼看劍尖（圖2–84）。

(7) Shift the weight to the left. The right foot steps to the left to form a Left Crossover Step. As the right foot touching the ground, the left foot pushes the ground. Bend the left leg and lift the foot backward behind the right lower leg, toes pointing down 10cm from the ground. Turn the upper body to the right slightly. At the same time, the right hand holds the sword and follows the body to draw an arc clockwise. The right hand stops in front of the body, wrist at chest level, arm bent and palm facing up. The tip of the sword is pointing to the right front. Move the left Sword Fingers in front of the body and place it on the inside of the right wrist, palm facing down. Eyes look at the

tip of the sword (Figure 2–84).

8. 左腳向左偏前上步，成左弓步，上體略左轉。同時，右手握劍向左抹劍，手心向上；左手劍指向左畫弧後，臂呈弧形舉於頭前左上方，眼看劍尖（圖2–85）。

(8) The left foot steps to the left front to form a Left Bow Step. Turn the upper body to the left slightly. At the same time, the right hand holds the sword and slides to the left

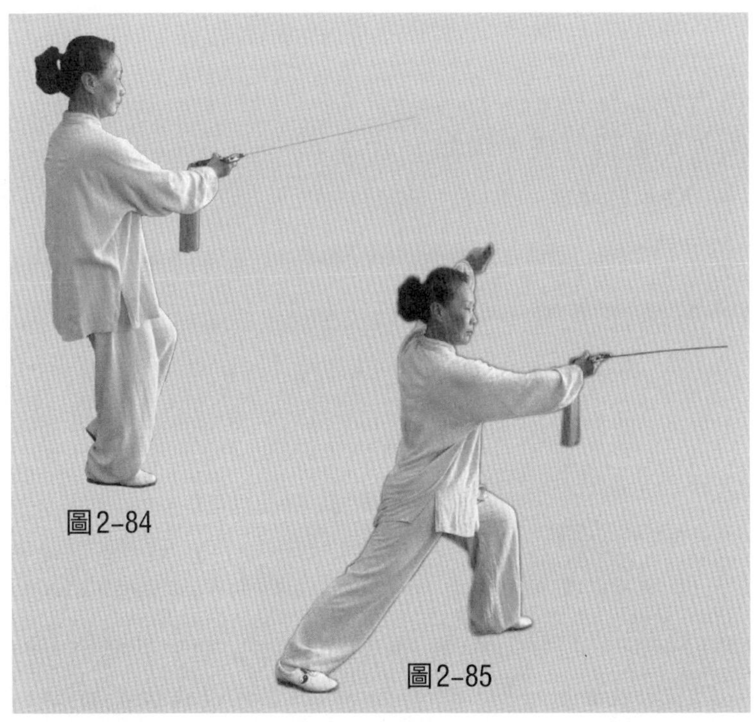
圖2–84 圖2–85

front, palm facing up. Move the left Sword Fingers to the left in an arc and the arm is arched over the left side of the head. Eyes look at the tip of the sword (Figure 2-85).

【要領】

(1) 步法變換要輕靈、平穩，重心移動要充分，虛實分明。

(2) 雲抹劍時以身帶劍，身隨步轉，眼隨劍走；劍的運行要連貫圓活，身劍協調，輕柔活潑。

【攻防含義】

若對方以劍刺我喉部，我以劍貼其劍向右（左）帶化後，即蓋步近身，同時雲劍繞到對方的右（左）側，抹斬對方腰、肋部。

Key Points

(1) Step gently and evenly. Shift the weight fully. Distinguish emptiness from solidness.

(2) When sliding the sword, the body follows the steps. Eyes follow the sword. Move the sword smoothly. Unite the sword and your body as one.

Application

If an opponent thrusts his sword towards your throat, move your sword and push his to the right or left, then step forward and move your sword to the right or left side of the opponent to slide his waist or ribs.

二十九、右弓步劈

1. 重心前移，上體左轉，右腳跟至左腳內側不觸地。同時，右手握劍向左畫弧帶至左腹前，手心斜向上，劍尖向左後下方；左手劍指屈肘向下落於右前臂上方，手心向下，眼看劍尖方向（圖2-86）。

29. Chop in Right Bow Step

(1) Shift the weight forward. Turn the upper body to the left. Bring the right foot and place it beside the left foot without touching the ground. At the same time, the right hand holds the sword and moves it to the left side of the abdomen, palm

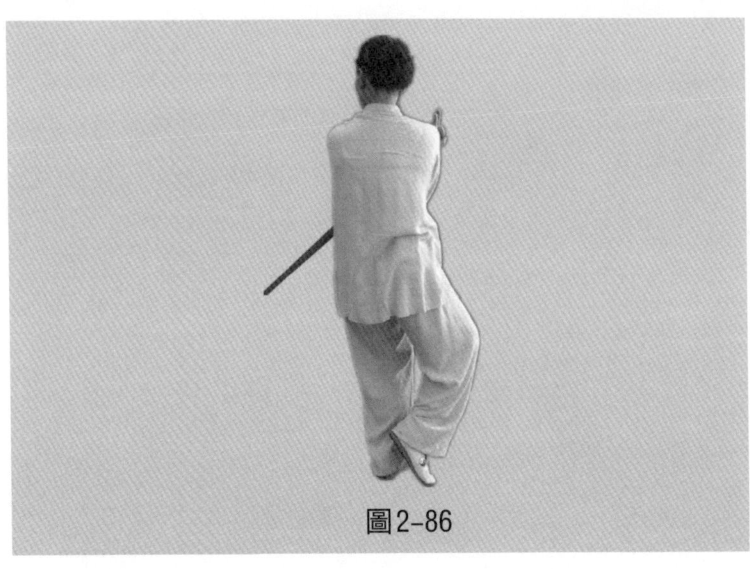

圖2-86

facing up diagonally. The tip of the sword is pointing lower left back. Bend the left elbow and move the left Sword Fingers down to the inside of the right forearm, palm facing down forward. Eyes look at the tip of the sword (Figure 2–86).

2. 右腳向右前方上步，上體右轉成右弓步。同時，右手握劍內旋，手心轉向外，經上向後畫弧劈劍，腕同胸平，左手劍指經下向左畫弧舉於頭左上方，眼看劍尖方向（圖2–87）。

(2) The right foot steps to the right front. Turn the upper body to the right to form a Right Bow Step. At the same time, the right hand rotates inward to turn the palm to face outward and chops down with the sword to the back in an arc, wrist at

圖2–87

chest level. Move the left Sword Fingers to draw an arc to above the left side of the forehead. Eyes look at the tip of the sword (Figure 2–87).

【要領】

（1）弓步、劈劍要協調一致，速度要均勻緩慢，動作圓活連貫，勁貫劍身。

（2）弓步劈劍方向在右前方，臂與劍身要平直一線。

【攻防含義】

若對方劍擊我左腿，我以劍向下向左後帶化，繼而上右步進身以劍向對方頭部劈擊。

Key Points

(1) The Bow Step and the chop are coordinated and finished at the same time. Move continuously, smoothly and evenly. Deliver the force to the sword.

(2) Chop to the right front, which is the same direction as the Bow Step. The arm and sword are aligned.

Application

If an opponent thrusts his sword towards your left leg, push his sword down and to the left back with your own, and then step forward to chop at his head.

三十、後舉腿架劍

1. 身體重心前移，左腳尖外擺向前蓋步屈膝半蹲，右腳跟提起，身體微左轉。同時，右手握劍內旋，手心向裏，向左掛劍，腕與腰齊平，左手劍指屈肘落於右前臂上方，眼看左下方（圖2-88）。

30. Parry and Kick Backward

(1) Shift the weight forward. Swing the left toes outward and the left foot steps forward and bend in a half squat to form a Crossover Step. Lift the right foot. Turn the upper body to the left slightly. At the same time, the right hand rotates inward and stabs back with the sword, palm facing inward. The tip of the sword is pointing left, wrist at waist level. Bend the left elbow and move the left Sword Fingers above the right forearm. Eyes look the lower front (Figure 2-88).

2. 左腿緩緩自然直立支撐重心，右腿屈膝後舉小腿，腳面展平與臀同高。同時，上體微左轉，隨之右手握劍內旋，手心轉向外，向上架舉，劍身距頭10公分，劍尖向左；左手劍指經頭前向左側舉，手心向外，劍指向上，眼看劍指方向（圖2-89）。

(2) The left leg stands up and supports the weight. Bend the right leg and lift the lower leg backward, stretch the foot at

buttock level. At the same time, turn the upper body to the left slightly. The right hand rotates inward to turn the palm to face outward and lifts the sword over the forehead. The sword is 10cm from the head, tip pointing left. Move the left Sword Fingers across the head to the left, palm facing outward, fingers pointing up. Eyes look at the left hand (Figure 2–89).

【要領】

（1）左手劍指與劍尖為同一方向，回頭眼向劍指方向看。

（2）後舉腿、舉劍上架、劍指指出要協調一致。

（3）獨立要穩，上體略前傾並略向左轉，支撐重

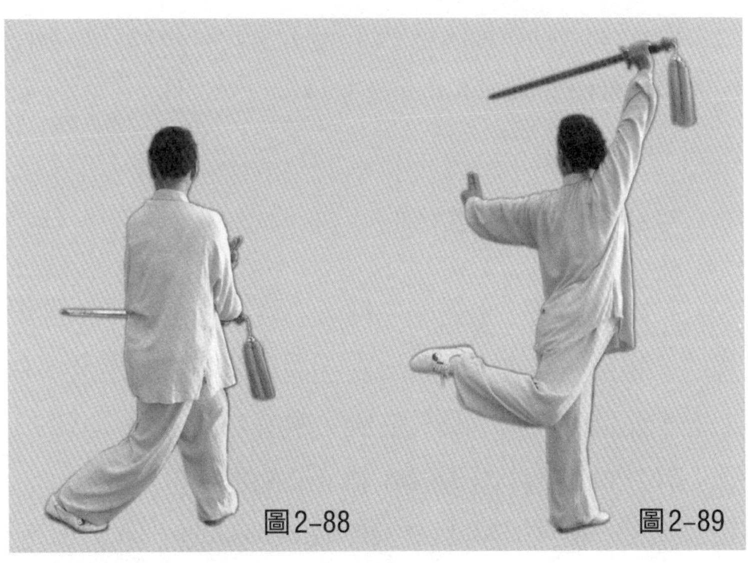

圖2–88　圖2–89

心的左腿要鬆膝、胯鬆、氣沉。

【攻防含義】

若對方從左側以劍向我頭劈來，我則以劍上架擋其劈劍，同時後舉腿，以腳撩踢對方腹部或襠部。

Key Points

(1) The left Sword Fingers point the same direction with the tip of the sword. Turn the head to look at the left Sword Fingers.

(2) Lifting the leg backward and lifting the sword should be coordinated with the Sword Fingers.

(3) Stand on the left leg steadily; relax the knee and hip. Sink the energy. Lean the upper body forward slightly and turn it a little to the left.

Application

If an opponent chops at your head, lift your sword to parry it. At the same time, lift the leg backward to kick his abdomen or crotch.

三十一、丁步點劍

1. 左腿屈膝，上體略右轉；右腳向右前落步，腳跟著地，腿自然伸直。同時，右手握劍略向右擺舉至頭右上方，使劍尖向上，高於右腕，眼看左前方(圖2-90)。

31. Point Sword Down in T-Step

(1) Bend the left knee and turn the upper body to the

right. The right foot steps to the right front, heel on ground, leg extended. At the same time, the right hand holds the sword and moves over the right side of the forehead. The tip of the sword is higher than the wrist, tip pointing up. Eyes look at the left front (Figure 2-90).

2. 重心右移於右腿，身體右轉，右腳踏實，屈膝半蹲；左腳跟至右腳內側，腳尖點地成左丁步。同時，右手握劍向右點擊，腕與胸同高，左手劍指經體前向右畫弧屈肘後附於右腕內側，眼看劍尖（圖2-91）。

(2) Shift the weight onto the right leg and turn the upper body to the right. Place the right foot on the ground firmly.

圖2-90 圖2-91

Bend the leg in a half squat. The left foot follows to the inside of the right foot, toes touching the ground to form a T-shape Step. At the same time, the right hand holds the sword and points down to the right, wrist at chest level. The left Sword Fingers draw an arc in front of the body to the right and rest on the inside of the right wrist, the elbow bent. Eyes look at the tip of the sword (Figure 2-91).

【要領】

（1）丁步與點劍要協調一致，同時完成。

（2）點劍要提腕，力達劍鋒，避免做成劈劍。

【攻防含義】

若對方以劍刺我左腰，我右轉身閃開，並進身跟步，以劍尖點擊對方腕部。

Key Points

(1) The T-Shape Step is coordinated with pointing the sword; they are both finished at the same time.

(2) When pointing the sword down, raise the wrist and deliver the force to the tip; do not make it a chop.

Application

If an opponent thrusts his sword at your left waist, turn your body to the right and dodge it, then step forward and stab his wrist with the tip of your sword.

三十二、馬步推劍

1. 左腳向左後方撤步，右腿屈膝，隨重心後移，以腳掌擦地撤半步，腳跟提起，腿微屈，上體向右擰轉。同時，右手握劍，虎口向上，屈肘收至右肋下，劍身豎直，劍尖向上；左手劍指附於右腕，手心向下，眼看右側（圖2-92）。

32. Push Sword in Horse Step

(1) The left foot steps backward. Bend the right leg. As the weight is shifting backward, the right forefoot sweeps a half step backward, the heel off the ground, the leg bent slightly. The upper body twists to the right slightly. At the same time, the right hand holds the sword, the tiger mouth facing up, the

圖2-92

arm bent at the lower side of the right ribs. The sword is upright, tip pointing up. The left Sword Fingers rest on the right wrist, palm facing downward. Eyes look at the right (Figure 2-92).

2. 左腳蹬地，隨身體重心前移，右腳向右前方上步，腳尖微內扣，左腳跟滑半步，兩腿屈膝半蹲成馬步，上體左轉。同時，右手握劍向右前方立劍平推，腕同胸齊平，劍尖向上，力貫劍身前刃；左手劍指經胸前向左推舉，手心向外，指尖向上，與肩同高，眼看右方（圖2-93）。

(2) The left foot pushes the ground. As the weight is shifting forward, the right foot steps to the right front, toes pointing inward slightly. The left foot slides a half step. Bend both legs

圖2-93

in a half squat to form a Horse Step. Turn the upper body to the left. At the same time, the right hand holds the sword and pushes to the right front with the sword upright, wrist at chest level. The tip of the sword is pointing upward, delivering the force to the front edge. Push the left Sword Fingers past in front of the chest to the left, palm facing outward, fingers pointing up at shoulder level. Eyes look at the right (Figure 2-93).

【要領】

（1）馬步與推劍要協調一致，同時完成，不可先馬步後推劍。

（2）此勢為發力動作，要以腰帶劍，轉腰收劍，要鬆腰鬆胯，加大右擰幅度，沉氣蓄勁。轉腰推劍時要沉胯呼氣，勁由腰發，眼隨劍走，勁力順達。

【攻防含義】

若對方以劍刺我胸，我速撤步右轉，豎劍貼住對方劍向右掛帶，繼而順其劍搶步進身，以劍身推割對方握劍之手。

Key Points

(1) Pushing sword is coordinated with the Horse Step and they are both finished at the same time.

(2) This movement is forceful. Use the waist to lead the sword. Turn the waist to bring back the sword. Relax the waist

and the hip. Make a big turn to the right. Sink the energy and gather the force. When turning the body and pushing the sword out, sink the hip and exhale. The force comes from the waist and is released smoothly. Eyes follow the sword.

Application

If an opponent thrusts his sword toward your chest, step backward and turn to the right. Hold your sword against his and push it to the right. Then step forward and use your sword to push his hand, which is holding the sword.

第四組

三十三、獨立上托

1. 身體重心左移，右腳向左插步，身體右轉。同時，右手握劍以腕為軸，外旋翻轉手腕，使劍尖經下向後向上在體右側立圓畫弧至頭右側，劍尖向右上方，虎口仍向上，腕同胸高，左手劍指略向前擺舉，眼看右前方（圖2–94）。

Group 4

33. Lift Sword over Head in One Leg Standing

(1) Shift the weight to the left. The right foot steps to the left back in Crossover Backward Step. Turn the body to the right. Meanwhile, using the wrist as the axle, turn over the right

hand and move the tip of the sword backward and downward at the right side of the body, drawing a vertical ellipse to the right side of the head. Meanwhile, the tip of the sword points to the upper right, the "tiger mouth" facing up and the wrist at chest level. Lift the left Sword Fingers forward slightly. Eyes look to the right front (Figure 2-94).

2. 隨身體重心後移，兩腿屈膝下蹲，並以左腳跟、右腳掌為軸碾步，向右後轉體180°。同時，右手握劍前臂內旋，劍柄領先向下向右後方畫弧擺舉至右膝前上方，劍尖向前；左手劍指屈肘向右附於右腕內側，手心向下，眼看劍尖（圖2-95）。

(2) While shifting the weight backward, bend the knees

圖2-94　圖2-95

in a half squat. Pivoting on the left heel and the right forefoot, turn the body 180° to the right. Meanwhile, turn the right forearm inward, with the hilt ahead, move the sword downward and then to the right back in an arc to the upper front of the right knee, the tip pointing forward. The left Sword Fingers move to the right to touch the inside of the wrist by bending the elbow, palm facing down. Eyes look at the tip of sword (Figure 2–95).

3. 上體略右轉，右腿自然直立，左腿屈膝提起成右獨立步。同時，右手握劍臂內旋上舉停於右額上方約10公分處，劍身平直，劍尖向左；左手劍指屈肘附於右前臂內側，手心向外，眼向左看（圖2–96）。

(3) Turn the upper body to the right. The right leg stands

圖2–96

naturally straight. Bend the left knee and lift it to form a One Leg Stand. At the same time, turn the right arm inward and lift the sword about 10 cm over the right side of the forehead, the blade flat and the tip pointing left. Place the left Sword Fingers onto the inside of the right forearm, palm facing outward. Eyes look to the left (Figure 2-96).

【要領】

（1）插步轉體時，上體不可過於前俯，不可凸臀，保持上體基本正直，斂臀，沉氣。

（2）提膝與上舉劍要配合協調，同時完成；保持獨立平穩。

（3）獨立上托方向與馬步推劍相反。

【攻防含義】

若對方以劍劈我頭，我起身獨立，以劍身將對方劈劍向上托架。

Key Points

(1) When turning the body in Thrust Step, do not bend the upper body too much forward or push the buttocks out. Keep the upper body basically upright. Pull in the buttocks and sink the energy.

(2) Lifting the knee and raising the sword should be coordinated with each other and finished at the same time. Keep the

One Leg Stand stable.

(3) The direction that one faces for Lift Sword over Head in One Leg Standing is opposite to "Push Sword in Horse Step".

Application

If the opponent chops down at your head with a sword, stand on one leg and lift the incoming sword upward with the blade of your sword.

三十四、進步掛劍

1. 左腳向左擺步，隨身體重心前移，右腳跟提起，上體略左轉。同時，右手握劍向左下方畫弧掛劍，手心向裏；左手劍指屈肘附於右臂內側，手心向外，眼看劍尖方向（圖2-97）。

34. Step Up and Stab Back

(1) The left foot steps to the left in a Toes Out Step. While shifting the weight forward, lift the right heel and turn the upper body to the left slightly. Meanwhile, the right hand stabs the sword to the lower left in an arc, palm facing inward. Bend the left elbow to place the left Sword Fingers to the inside of the right upper arm, palm facing out. Eyes look at the tip of the sword (Figure 2-97).

2. 隨身體重心前移，右腳擺步向前，上體略右轉。同時，右手握劍經上向前畫弧，前臂外旋，手心向上，劍尖向前，低於右腕；左手劍指仍附於右前臂內側，手心向右，眼看劍尖方向（圖2-98）。

（2）While shifting the weight forward, the right foot steps forward in a Toes Out Step. Turn the upper body to the right slightly. At the same time, move the sword forward in an arc with the forearm turned outward and palm facing up; the tip of the sword points to the front, and is lower than the wrist. The left Sword Fingers remain on the inside of the right forearm, palm facing to the right. Eyes look at the tip of the sword (Figure 2-98).

3. 重心前移，右腳踏實，左腳跟提起，上體略右

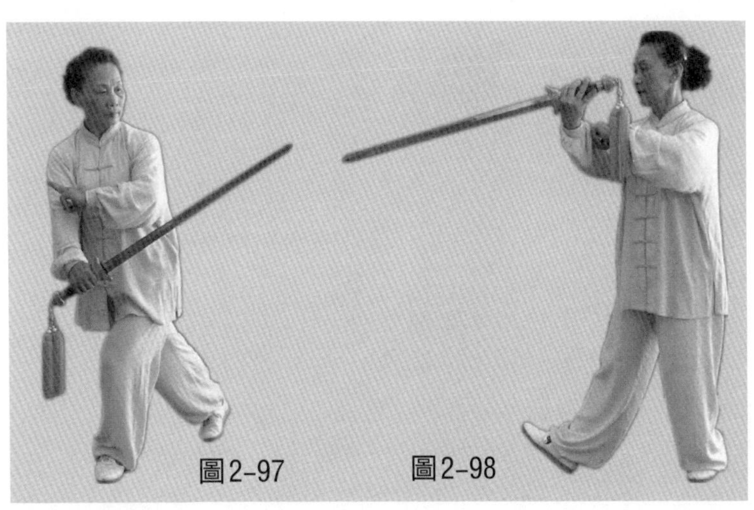
圖2-97 圖2-98

轉。同時，右手握劍向右畫弧穿掛劍，手心向外；左手劍指向上，臂呈弧形舉至頭上方，手心向左，眼看劍尖方向（圖2-99）。

(3) Shift the weight forward. Place the right foot on the ground solidly. Lift the left heel, and turn the upper body to the right slightly. Meanwhile, the right hand draws an arc to stabs the sword to the right, palm facing up. The left Sword Fingers rise above the head, arm arched and palm facing left. Eyes look at the tip of the sword (Figure 2-99).

4. 重心前移，左腳擺步向前，腳跟著地，身體略左轉。同時，右手握劍向右伸舉，手心向上，腕同腰高，劍尖向右下方；左手劍指下落至與肩同高，手心

圖2-99

向外，眼看劍指方向（圖2-100）。

(4) Shift the weight forward. The left foot steps forward in a Toes Out Step, only the heel touching the ground. Turn the body to the left slightly. Meanwhile, the right hand holds out the sword to the right, palm facing up, the wrist at waist level, and the tip pointing to the lower right. The Sword Fingers fall down to the level of the shoulders, palm facing outward. Eyes look at the Sword Fingers (Figure 2-100).

5. 身體重心前移，左腳踏實，屈膝半蹲，右腳向右前方上步成右虛步，上體左轉約90°。同時，右手握劍經上向右前下方點劍，左手劍指經下向左畫弧，臂呈弧形舉至頭左上方，手心斜上，眼看劍尖（圖2- 101）。

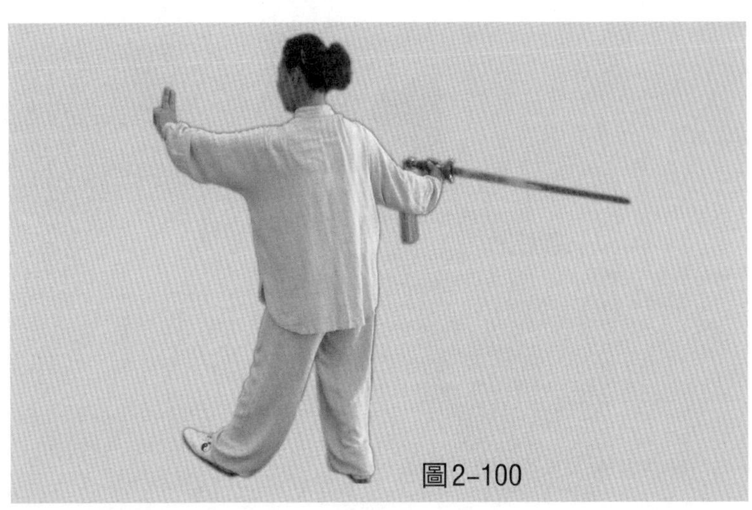
圖2-100

(5) Shift the weight forward. Place the left foot on the ground solidly and bend the knee in a half squat. The right foot takes a step to the right front to form a Right Empty Step. Turn the upper body about 90° to the left. Meanwhile, point the sword to the lower right front. The left Sword Fingers draw an arc to the left and then upward to the upper left of the head, arm arched and palm facing diagonally up. Eyes look at the tip of the sword (Figure 2-101).

【要領】

(1) 左右掛劍動作要連貫圓活、貼近身體，立圓掛劍；虛步與點劍要協調一致，同時完成。

(2) 上步掛劍、點劍前進方向與獨立架劍方向

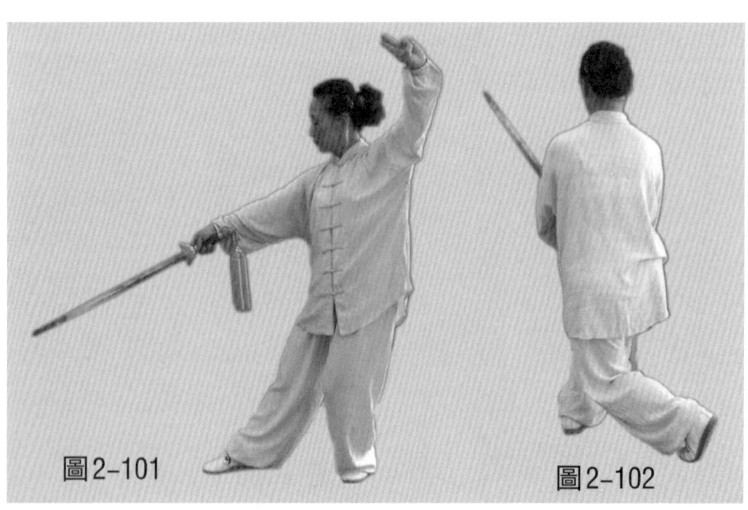
圖2-101　圖2-102

一致。

【攻防含義】

若對方以劍刺我下盤，我以劍向左（右）掛帶化開，並上步進身，以劍點擊對方頭或腕。

Key Points

(1) The stabs should be continuous, smooth, and close to the body. Move the sword in a vertical ellipse. The Empty Step and pointing the sword should be coordinated with each other and finished at the same time.

(2) The direction of the stepping up and pointing the sword is the same as that of the One Leg Stand step and lifting up the sword.

Application

If the opponent thrust his sword to your lower body, you can stab the sword to the left or right to lead it away and then step forward to stab his head or wrist.

三十五、歇步崩劍

1. 右腳輕提外擺踏實並屈膝半蹲，身體重心前移，上體右轉。同時，右手握劍翹腕向後帶劍至右胯旁，手心向內，劍尖向左上方，略低於肩；左手劍指屈肘下落附於右腕上，手心向下，眼看右前下方（圖2-102）。

35. Burst in Low Squat with Crossed Legs

(1) Lift the right foot slightly, swing it outward, and place it on the ground solidly while bending the knee in a half squat. Shift the weight forward and turn the upper body to the right. At the same time, lift the right wrist and withdraw the sword to the right side of the hip, palm facing inward; the tip of the sword points to the upper left, slightly lower than the shoulder. Bend the left arm and rest the left Sword Fingers on the right wrist, palm facing down. Eyes look at the lower right front (Figure 2-102).

2. 身體重心略左移，右腿屈膝，左腳向左上步，上體右轉，成右弓步。同時，右手握劍經下向右畫弧反撩，腕同胸齊平，手心向後，劍尖向右；左手劍指經下向左畫弧擺舉至與肩平，眼看劍尖（圖2-103）。

(2) Shift the weight to the left slightly. Bend the right knee. The left foot takes a step to the left. Turn the upper body to the right to form a Right Bow Step. Meanwhile, the right hand moves the sword in a downward arc to the right with palm facing back, the tip of the sword pointing to the right, and the wrist at waist level. The left Sword Fingers draw an arc to the left and then upward to shoulder level. Eyes look at the tip of the sword (Figure 2-103).

3. 重心後移至左腿，右腳向左腳後撤步下蹲成歇步，身體右轉。同時，右手握劍，變虎口向上沉腕向上崩劍，腕同腰齊平；左手劍指向上畫弧上舉，臂呈弧形舉於左上方，手心斜向上，眼看右前方（圖2-104）。

(3) Shift the weight onto the left leg. The right foot steps backward, behind the left foot. Squat lower with crossed legs. Meanwhile, turn the "tiger mouth" of the right hand upward and sink the wrist to burst the sword up, the wrist at waist level. The left Sword Fingers draw an arc to the upper left, arm

圖2-103

圖2-104

arched and palm facing diagonally up. Eyes look to the right front (Figure 2–104).

【要領】

（1）歇步與崩劍動作要協調配合，同時完成。

（2）崩劍虎口向上，鬆肩沉腕，劍尖上崩，勁貫劍尖上鋒。

（3）上步、插步方向要一致。

【攻防含義】

若對方以劍刺我右胸，我右轉閃開其劍，並歇步下蹲沉腕以劍尖崩擊對方握劍之腕。

Key points

(1) The Crossed Leg Step should be coordinated with the bursting and finished at the same time.

(2) When bursting up, turn the "tiger mouth" to face up; relax the shoulder; sink the wrist. The tip of the sword is tilted up with a burst, the force delivered to its upper edge.

(3) The directions of the Bow Step and Crossover Backward Step are the same.

Application

If the opponent attacks your right chest with a sword, you can shift to the right to avoid it and attack his wrist, which is holding the sword, by sinking your wrist to burst the sword up

in a low squat with Crossed Legs.

三十六、弓步反刺

1. 右腳踏實，右腿伸展直立；左腿屈膝提起，腳尖下垂，上體稍左傾。同時，右手握劍屈肘側舉，腕低於胸，使劍身斜置於右肩上方，手心向外，劍尖向左上方；左手劍指下落，與肩同高，眼看右前方（圖2-105）。

36. Thrust Back in Bow Step

(1) Place the right foot on the ground solidly and extend the leg to stand straight. Bend the left leg and lift it up, with the toes hanging down and the upper body leaning to the left slightly. Meanwhile, bend the right elbow and raise the right

圖2-105

hand along the side to set the blade of the sword above the right shoulder, the wrist lower than the chest, the palm facing outward and the tip pointing the upper left. Move the left Sword Fingers down to shoulder level. Eyes look to the right front (Figure 2-105).

2. 左腳向左落步，成左弓步，上體略向左傾。同時，右手握劍向前上方探刺，左手劍指向右與右臂在體前相合，附於右前臂內側，眼看劍尖（圖2-106）。

(2) The left foot takes a step to the left to form a Left Bow Step. The upper body leans to the left slightly. At the same time, thrust the sword to the upper front. The left Sword Fingers move to the right to meet the right arm in front of the chest and

圖2-106

rest on the inside of the right forearm. Eyes look at the tip of the sword (Figure 2–106).

【要領】

（1）弓步與探刺要協調一致，動作舒展。

（2）左腳上步時，腳跟先著地，再成弓步；探刺時，右手握劍從右耳旁刺出，右臂前順，上臂貼近右耳，劍尖略高。

【攻防含義】

若對方以劍向我上盤右側刺擊，我側身帶化，隨即上步進身反刺對方頭部。

Key Points

(1) The Bow Step and the thrust should be coordinated with each other and the movements should be comfortable and stretched.

(2) When the left foot steps forward, place the heel on the ground first then the entire foot to form a Bow Step. While thrusting the sword, move the arm forward from the outside of the right ear naturally, the forearm close to the right ear and the tip of the sword higher than the blade.

Application

If the opponent uses the sword to attack the right side of your upper body or arms, step aside to lead his sword away then step forward to stab backward to the opponent's head.

三十七、轉身下刺

1. 重心向右腿移動，上體右轉，左腳尖內扣。同時，右手握劍屈肘回帶至左肩前，手心向裏，劍尖向右，劍身在面前10公分橫置；左手劍指附於右腕內側，手心向外，眼向右看（圖2-107）。

37. Turn Body Around and Thrust Down

(1) Shift the weight onto the right leg. Turn the upper body to the right. Swing the left toes inward. Meanwhile, the right hand holds the sword and moves back to the front of the left shoulder, palm facing inward and the tip of the sword pointing right. The blade of the sword is laid across the body, 10cm from the body. The left Sword Fingers stay on the inside of the right wrist, palm facing outward. Eyes look to the right (Figure 2-107).

2. 身體重心左移於左腿，右腿屈膝提起，腳尖下垂，以左腳掌為軸碾步，身體右轉。同時，右手握劍向右擺至右肩前，使劍尖向下畫弧至右膝外側，手心斜向外，劍尖斜向下，左手劍指仍附於右腕，眼看劍尖（圖2-108）。

(2) Shift the weight onto the left leg. Bend the right knee

and lift it up, the toes hanging down. Pivoting on the left fore-foot, turn the body to the right. Meanwhile, move the sword in front of the right shoulder and draw an arc with the tip of the sword downward to the outside of the right knee, palm facing diagonally outward and the tip pointing obliquely downward. The left Sword Fingers stay on the right wrist. Eyes look at the tip of the sword (Figure 2–108).

3. 上體右轉180°，左腳跟向左輾轉，右腳向右後方落步成右弓步。同時，右手握劍向弓步方向下平劍刺出，腕同腰齊平，劍尖與膝同高，手心向上；左手劍指仍附於右腕，手心向下，眼看劍尖（圖2–109）。

圖2–107　圖2–108

(3) Turn the upper body 180° to the right, pivoting on the left heel. The right foot steps to the right back to form a Right Bow Step. Meanwhile, the right hand thrusts the sword downward in the direction of the Bow Step with its blade flat, wrist at waist level, palm facing up, the tip of the sword at the height of the knee. The Sword Fingers stay on the right wrist, palm facing down. Eyes look at the tip of the sword (Figure 2-109).

【要領】

(1) 右腳向右後落步轉體時要先內扣左腳，再外展右腳，然後成弓步。

(2) 動作要連貫圓活，下刺後上體微前傾；弓步與刺劍要協調一致，呼氣助力。

圖2-109

【攻防含義】

若對方以劍由後刺我右腿，我提起右腿閃開，而後右轉身，上步進身，向對方下盤刺擊。

Key Points

(1) When turning the body and stepping to the right back, turn the left foot inward first and then extend the right foot to form a Bow Step.

(2) The movement should be continuous and smooth. When the sword is thrusting downward, the upper body leans forward slightly. The Bow Step is coordinated with the thrusting. Exhale to increase the power.

Application

If the opponent thrust his sword to your right leg from behind, lift the right leg to dodge it then turn to the right and step forward to thrust your sword towards his lower body.

三十八、提膝提劍

1. 身體重心後移，上體左轉；左腳尖外擺，屈膝半蹲，右腿自然伸直。同時，右手握劍，以劍柄領先，屈臂外旋，向左上方帶劍至離頭部20公分處，手心向裏，劍尖向右；左手劍指附於右前臂內側，手心向外，眼看劍尖（圖2-110）。

38. Raise Sword with the Tip Down and Lift the Knee

(1) Shift the weight backwards. Turn the upper body to the left. Turn the left toes outward and bend the knee in a half squat. Extend the right leg naturally straight. Meanwhile, bend the right arm and rotate it outward, withdrawing the sword to the upper left 20cm from the head, the hilt ahead, the tip pointing right, and palm facing inward. Place the left Sword Fingers to the inside of the right forearm, palm facing outward. Eyes look at the tip of sword(Figure 2–110).

2. 身體重心右移，右腿屈膝，左腿自然伸直，左腳跟外碾，上體略右轉。同時，右手握劍，劍柄領先，前臂內旋，手心向下，經腹前擺至右胸前，距胸30公分，使劍尖經上向右前畫弧，劍尖低於腕；左手劍指附於右腕內側，手心向外，眼看劍尖（圖2–111）。

(2) Shift the weight to the right. Bend the right leg. Extend the left leg naturally straight while pivoting on the heel outward. Turn the upper body to the right slightly. Meanwhile, rotate the right forearm inward, palm facing down, and swing the sword from the abdomen to the front of right chest 30cm from the chest. Draw an arc to the upper right with the tip of the sword, the tip lower than the wrist. Place the left Sword

Fingers on the inside of the right wrist, palm facing outward. Eyes look at the tip of the sword (Figure 2-111).

3. 左腿屈膝提起成右獨立步，上體略右轉並稍前傾。同時，右手握劍，劍柄領先，向右向上畫弧提劍，臂呈弧形舉於右前方，腕同頭高，虎口斜向下，劍尖置於左膝外側；左手劍指經腹前向左畫弧擺舉，與腰同高，手心向外，眼看左前下方（圖2-112）。

(3) Bend the left knee and lift it to form a One Leg Stand. Turn the upper body to the right slightly and lean forward slightly. At the same time, with the hilt ahead, the right hand draws the sword in an arc to the right front, the arm arched, the wrist at the head level, the "tiger mouth" facing diagonally

圖2-110 圖2-111

down. The tip of the sword is at the outside of the left knee. Swing the left Sword Fingers to the left in an arc past the abdomen to the left at waist level, palm facing outward. Eyes look to the lower left front (Figure 2–112).

【要領】

（1）提膝與提劍要協調一致。提劍不可聳肩、掀肘。

（2）提膝時，左腳向裏護襠，膝高不低於腰。

（3）獨立要平穩，要沉肩鬆胯，兩手對拉。

【攻防含義】

若對方以劍從左後刺擊我左腿，我左腿提起閃開，劍經上畫弧繞至對方右側由下向上提劍，截割對

圖2–112　圖2–113

方腕部。

Key Points

(1) Lifting the knee should be coordinated with raising the sword. Do not raise the shoulder or turn the elbow outward while raising the sword.

(2) While lifting the knee, the left foot points inward to protect the crotch, the knee higher than the waist.

(3) The One Leg Stand should be stable. Relax the shoulders and hips. Push hands in opposite directions.

Applications

If the opponent thrust his sword toward your leg from the left back, lift your left leg to dodge it, then wield your sword in an arc to the right side of the opponent and cut his wrist.

三十九、進步穿劍

1. 右腿屈膝，左腳向左前落步，腳跟著地。上體左轉時右手握劍，手心翻轉向上，劍尖領先，經左肋下向左向前穿劍，腕與腰齊平，劍尖向前；左手劍指向右上方畫弧擺舉至右肩前，手心向下，眼看劍尖（圖2-113）。

39. Thrust and Marching

(1) Bend the right leg. The left foot takes a step to the left front only the heel touching the ground. While turning the

upper body to the left, turn over the right hand to make the palm facing up. With the tip ahead, thrust the sword past the beneath of the left ribs to the left front, wrist at waist level, the tip of the sword pointing to the front. The left Sword Fingers draw an arc to the upper right and stop in front of the right shoulder, palm facing down. Eyes look at the tip of the sword (Figure 2-113).

2. 身體重心前移，左腳踏實，膝微屈，右腳弧形向右擺步，上體右轉。同時，右手握劍，劍尖領先，向前向右畫弧穿劍，腕與胸齊平，劍尖向右；左手劍指經胸前向右分展側舉，臂呈弧形，手心向外，眼看劍尖（圖2-114）。

(2) Shift the weight forward. Place the left foot on the ground solidly, the knee bent slightly. Swing the right toes to the right in a Toes Out Step. Turn the upper body to the right. At the same time, with the tip ahead, the right hand thrusts the sword right front in an arc, the tip pointing right and the wrist at chest level. Move the left Sword Fingers past the chest to the right of the body, arm arched and palm facing out. Eyes look at the tip of the sword (Figure 2-114).

3. 隨身體重心前移，左腳向右扣步，上體繼續右轉，兩手動作不變（圖2-115）。

(3) With shifting the weight forward, swing the left toes inward in a Toes In Step. Turn the upper body to the right. Keep the hands in the same positions (Figure 2-115).

4. 重複2與3，右腳、左腳各上步，兩手動作不變。

(4) Repeat (2) and (3), the right foot and the left foot take a step forward respectively. Keep the hands in the same positions.

【要領】

（1）穿劍時，要沉胯、擰腰、鬆肩，墜肘蓄勁，眼看劍尖，劍追進尾閭。

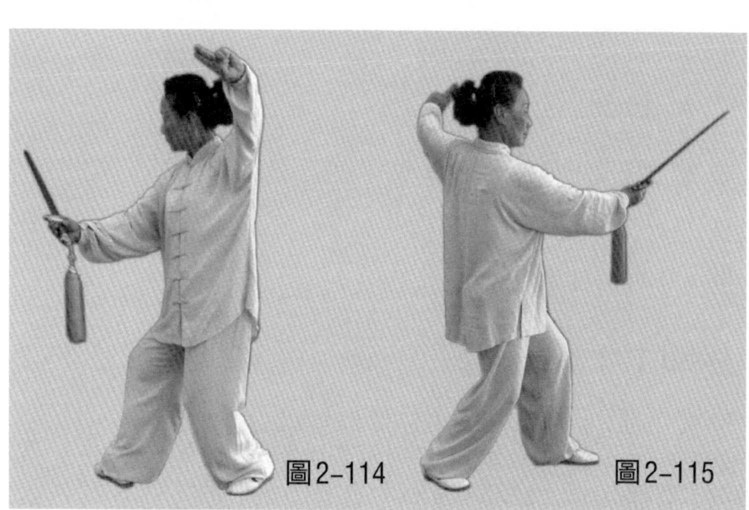

圖2-114　圖2-115

（2）進步時，左腳扣，右腳擺，行走平穩、連貫，不可飄浮，上體不要上下起伏。共走5步，軌跡為一個圓形。

【攻防含義】

若對方以劍刺我胸，我向左落步閃身，同時以劍穿至對方右側，掛穿其握劍之手腕。

Key Points

(1) While thrusting the sword, sink the hips, twist the waist and relax the shoulders. Sink the elbows to gather the force. Eyes look at the tip of the sword. The sword follows the tail bone.

(2) When stepping forward, the left foot turns inward and the right foot turns outward; the steps should be stable, continuous, do not sway; do not move the upper body up and down. The five steps form a circular track.

Applications

If the opponent thrusts his sword at your chest, you can step to the left to dodge it and thrust your sword at his wrist, which is holding the sword.

四十、擺腿架劍

1. 右手握劍，前臂內旋經面前使劍尖在頭前方逆時針畫弧，屈肘向左擺至左肋前，劍尖向左上方。當右手握劍左擺至頭前時，右腳外擺至右前方時屈小腿成左獨立步。左手劍指向上在面前與右手相合，屈肘附於右腕內側，手心向下，眼看前方（圖2-116、圖2-117）。

40. Parry with Lotus Kick

(1) By turning the forearm inward, the right hand holds the sword and draws a counter-clockwise arc with the tip in front of the head. Then bend the elbow and move the sword in front of the left ribs, the tip pointing to the upper left. When the right hand wields the sword left in front of the head, swing the right foot outward to the right front and bend the lower leg to form a One Leg Stand. The left Sword Fingers move up to meet the right hand in front of face and rest on the inside of the

圖2-116　圖2-117

right wrist by bending the elbow, palm facing down. Eyes look ahead (Figure 2–116, Figure 2–117).

2. 左腿屈膝，右腳向右前方落步，上體右轉。同時，右手握劍經前向右畫弧抹劍，腕與胸同高，手心向下，劍尖向左；左手劍指附於右前臂內側，手心向下，眼看劍身前端（圖2–118）。

(2) Bend the left leg. The right foot takes a step to the right front. Turn the upper body to the right. Meanwhile, the right hand holds the sword and slides it to the right in an arc across the front of the body, wrist at chest level, palm facing down and the tip of the sword pointing left. Place the left Sword Fingers on the inside of the right forearm, palm facing down. Eyes look at the front part of the blade of the sword (Figure 2–118).

3. 右腿屈膝半蹲，左腳跟外展成右弓步，上體左轉。同時，右手握劍上舉架劍，劍尖斜向前；左手劍指隨右手上舉後經面前向劍尖方向指出，指尖向上，高與鼻齊平，眼看劍尖方向（圖2–119）。

(3) Bend the right leg in a half squat. Turn the left heel outward to form a Right Bow Step. Turn the upper body to the left. At the same time, the right hand raises the sword, the tip

pointing forward diagonally. The left Sword Fingers, following the right hand, point in the same direction as the tip of the sword, fingertips pointing up at nose level. Eyes look at the tip of the sword (Figure 2-119).

【要領】

（1）外擺腿是扇形軌跡，高度不要低於胸（中老年者量力而行），並與劍和劍指動作協調配合。

（2）右腳下落時腳跟先著地，左腿屈膝，重心下降，上體不宜前移，而後再成右弓步，弓步架劍和前指配合完成。

【攻防含義】

若對方以劍向我頭部劈來，我則向右落步閃開，

圖2-118　圖2-119

以劍舉架對方劈劍，並以劍指攻擊對方面部。

Key points

(1) Swing the leg up in an arc no lower than the chest. (Senior people can finish it according their ability) The swing is coordinated with the sword and the Sword Fingers.

(2) When placing right foot on the ground, put the heel on the ground first then squat with the left leg and lower the weight. Do not move the upper body forward before to form the Right Bow Step. Lifting the sword should be coordinated with pointing the Sword Fingers.

Applications

If an opponent chops at your head with his sword, step to right to dodge it then lift your sword to push his sword upward and stab at his face with your Sword Fingers.

四十一、弓步直刺

1. 重心移至右腿，左腳收提至右腳內側，不可點地。同時，右手握劍經右下收至右胯旁，虎口向前，劍尖向前；左手劍指經左向下收至左胯旁，手心向下，指尖向前，眼看前方（圖2-120）。

41. Thrust Straight in Bow Step

(1) Shift the weight onto the right leg. Bring the left foot to the inside of the right leg without letting it touch the ground.

Meanwhile, the right hand withdraws the sword past the lower right to the right side of the hip, the "tiger mouth" facing forward and the tip of the sword pointing forward. Move the left Sword Fingers to the left side of the hip, palm facing down and fingertips pointing forward. Eyes look ahead (Figure 2–120).

2. 左腳向前上步，右腿自然伸直成左弓步。同時，右手握劍立刃向前平刺，左手劍指在胸前與右手相合，附於右腕內側後向前伸送，手心斜向下，眼看前方（圖2–121）。

(2) Move the left foot a step forward and bend the left knee. Extend the right leg naturally straight to form a Left Bow Step. At the same time, the right hand thrusts the sword

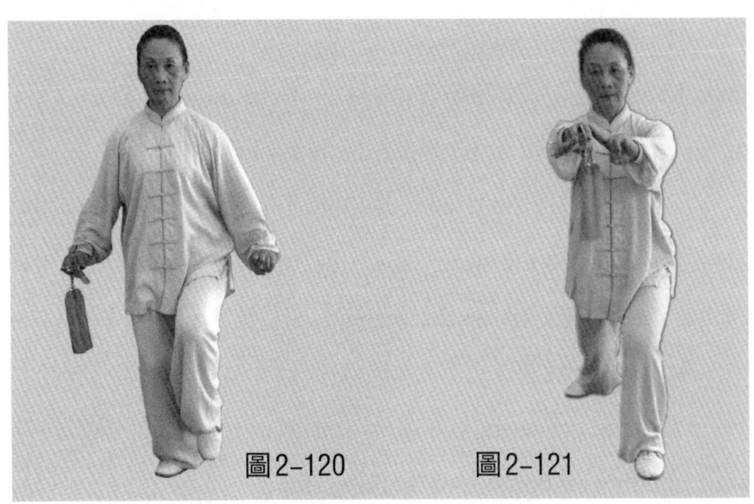

圖2–120　　圖2–121

straight forward with the edge up. The left Sword Fingers rest on the inside of the right hand in front of the chest and extend forward, palm facing down diagonally. Eyes look ahead (Figure 2-121).

【要領】

（1）上步時腳跟先著地，上體保持正直舒鬆，不可挺腹、凸臀。

（2）弓步與刺劍同時進行，刺劍要對準身體中線，不可偏右側。

【攻防含義】

對方迎面而來，我即迅速上步進身，以劍刺向對方。

Key Points

(1) When stepping forward, place the heel on the ground first. Keep the upper body upright and comfortable. Do not let the abdomen be stiff or push out the buttocks.

(2) The Bow Step and the thrusting are finished at the same time. While thrusting, align the tip of the sword with the centre of the body. Do not let it slant.

Applications

When an opponent comes at you from the front, step forward rapidly and thrust your sword at him.

四十二、收　式

1. 重心後移，右腿屈膝，上體右轉。同時，右手握劍屈肘向右回帶至右胸前，左手劍指仍附於右腕，隨之右收，兩手心相對，準備接劍，劍身微貼左前臂外側，眼看前方（圖2-122）。

42. Closing

(1) Shift the weight backward. Bend the right knee. Turn the upper body to the right. Meanwhile, bend the right elbow to bring the sword back to the right front of the chest. The left Sword Fingers stay on the right wrist and move with it, palms face each other. The left hand is ready to take over the sword. The blade of the sword clings to the outside of the left forearm. Eyes look ahead (Figure 2-122).

2. 上體左轉，重心前移，右腳上步與左腳成平行步。同時，左手劍指變掌接劍（反握），經前向左擺置於左胯旁，手心向後，劍身豎直，劍尖向上；右手變為劍指，經下向右後畫弧，隨屈肘舉至右耳旁，手心向內，指尖向上，眼看前方（圖2-123）。

(2) Turn the upper body to the left. Shift the weight forward. The right foot takes a step forward to be parallel to the left foot. Meanwhile, change the left Sword Fingers into an

open palm to take over the sword (in backhand). Swing the sword to the left and stop at the side of the left hip, palm facing back, the blade erected and the tip pointing up. The right hand, turning into Sword Fingers, draws an arc past the lower right to the back and stop at the side of the right ear, the elbow bent, palm facing inward and the fingertips pointing up. Eyes look ahead (Figure 2–123).

3. 兩腿自然伸直。同時，右手劍指經胸前向下落於身體右側，然後左腳向右腳併攏，身體自然站立，兩臂垂於體側，眼看前方（圖2–124、圖2–125）。

(3) Extend the legs naturally straight. Meanwhile, the right

圖2–122 圖2–123

Sword Fingers, across the front of the chest, fall down to the right side of the body. Bring the left foot together with the right foot. Stand straight naturally, the arms hanging down by the sides of the body. Eyes look ahead (Figure 2–124, Figure 2–125).

【要領】

（1）動作要連貫、圓活、緩慢。

（2）併步時，左腳要點起點落，全身放鬆，深呼氣，意氣回歸丹田。

（3）收式後，略停片刻再走動。

Key Points

(1) The movement should be continuous, smooth and slow.

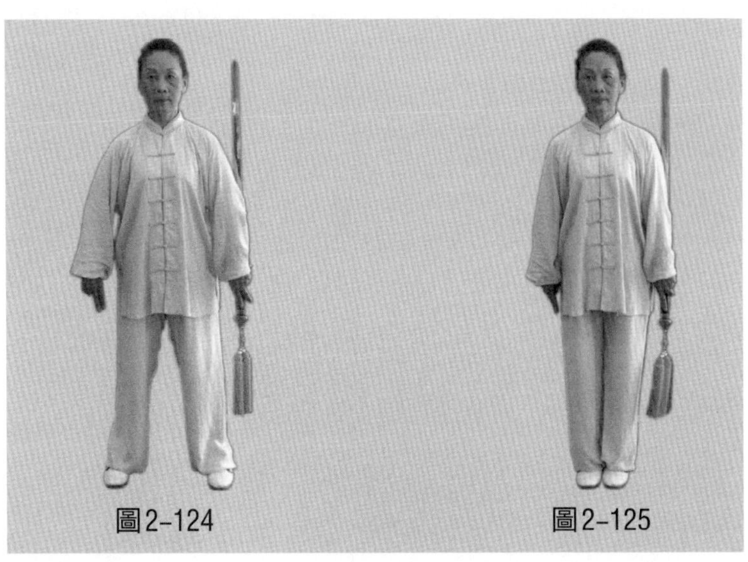

圖2-124　圖2-125

(2) When moving the feet together, lift the left heel first and place the toes on the ground first. Relax the entire body. Breathe deeply. Let the energy sink (Qi) and keep the mind on the Dantian (the lower abdomen).

(3) After completing the Closing, stay quiet for a moment before walking.

附　42式太極劍動作佈局路線圖

熟悉並掌握套路動作線路佈局變化十分重要，因為步法的變化，落腳之位置和方向，不僅影響套路演練的連貫性和美感，更重要的是它確保了每個招式的方向、位置和根基的穩固。

套路的練習目的不僅在於熟練動作，還包含了對肢體動作乃至招式之間的起承轉合的體悟，對於在攻防實踐中的運用招式有直接的影響，在增強表演觀賞效果方面也有重要的作用（見附圖）。

Appendix Path Map of the 42-form Tai Chi Sword Movements

It is important to understand the path of the TaiJi forms. The location, the direction, and the translation between the steps have a great impact on the coherence of the whole form. More important, the path provides a solid foundation for each movement. When practising, one should not only be familiar with the movements, but also understand the connection between the movements, which is more important when applying to attacking and defending (see the figure on Page 95).

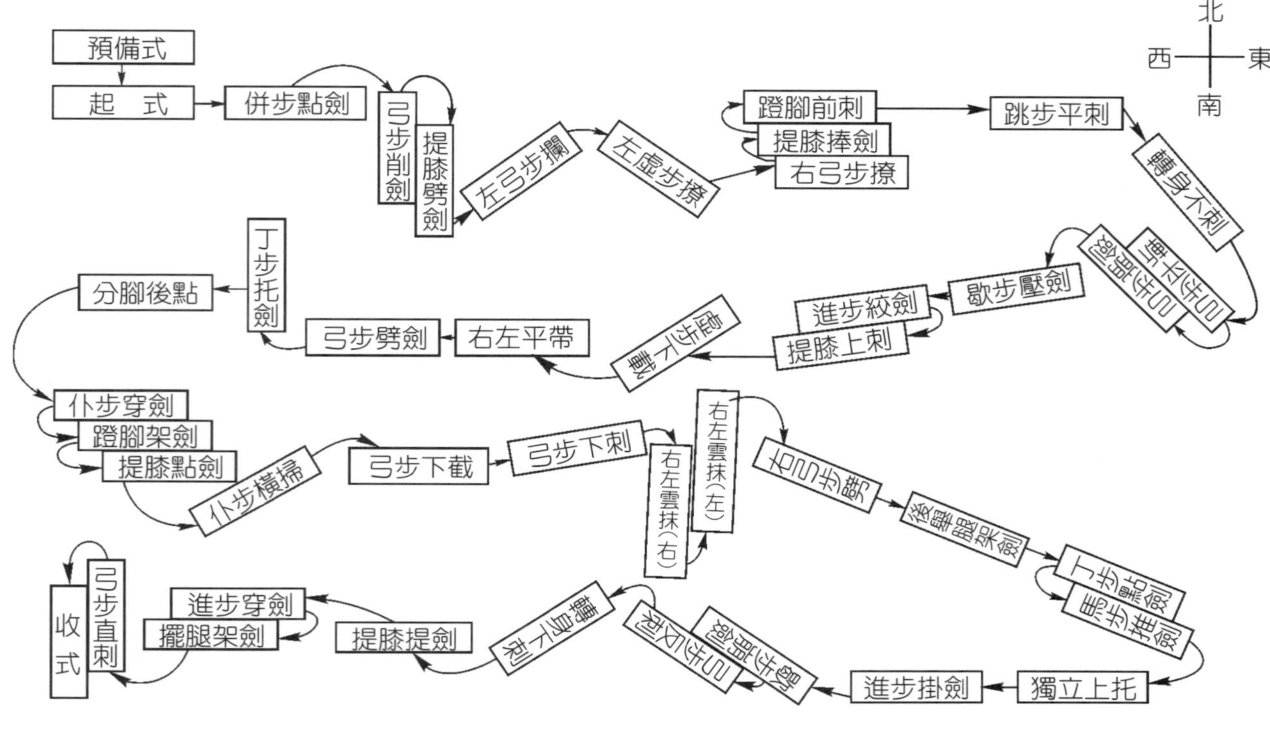
北
西
東
南
預備式
起　式
併步點劍
弓步削劍
提膝劈劍
左弓步攔
左虛步撩
右弓步撩
提膝捧劍
蹬腳前刺
跳步平刺
轉身下刺
弓步平斬
弓步崩劍
歇步壓劍
進步絞劍
提膝上刺
虛步下截
右左平帶
弓步劈劍
丁步托劍
分腳後點
仆步穿劍
蹬腳架劍
提膝點劍
仆步橫掃
弓步下截
弓步下刺
右左雲抹（右）
右左雲抹（左）
右弓步劈
後舉腿架劍
丁步點劍
馬步推劍
獨立上托
進步掛劍
歇步崩劍
弓步反刺
轉身下刺
提膝提劍
進步穿劍
擺腿架劍
弓步直刺
收式

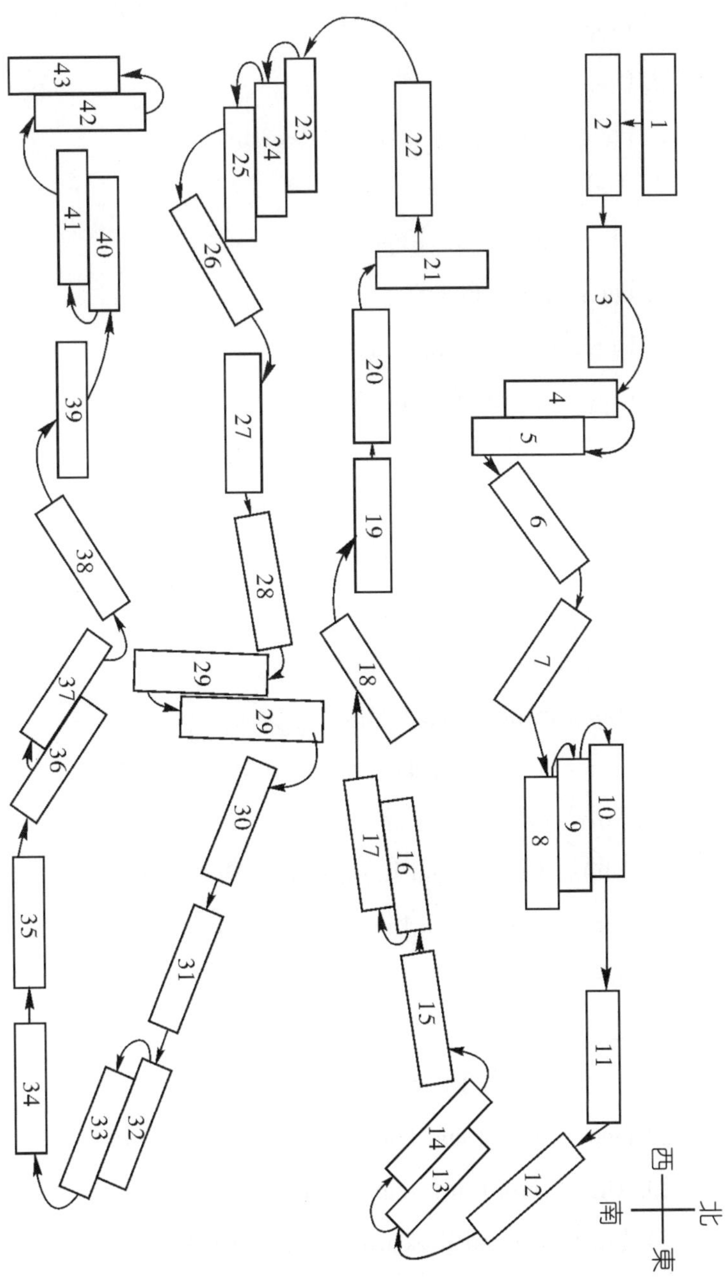

1
2
3
4
5
6
7
8
9
10
11
12
13
14
15
16
17
18
19
20
21
22
23
24
25
26
27
28
29
29
30
31
32
33
34
35
36
37
38
39
40
41
42
43
北
東
南
西

1. Preparation
2. Opening
3. Point Sword Down and Feet Together
4. Peel in Bow Step
5. Chop and Lift the Knee
6. Parry in Left Bow Step
7. Upward Slice in Left Empty Step
8. Upward Slice in Right Bow Step
9. Hold Sword with Both Hands and Lift the Knee
10. thrust Forward and Kick with the Heel
11. Jump and Thrust Flat
12. Turn Body and Thrust Down
13. Horizontal Slash in Bow Step
14. Burst in Bow Step
15. Pressing Sword in Low Squat with Crossing Legs
16. Stirring and Marching
17. Thrust Upward and Raise Knee
18. Intercept Downward in Empty Step
19. Withdraw Sword – Right and Left
20. Chop in Bow Step
21. Lift Sword in T – Step
22. Separate Foot and Point Sword Back
23. Thrust Sword in Crouch Step – Right
24. Lift Sword and Kick with the Left Heel

25. Point Sword Down and Lift the Left Knee
26. Swing Sword in Crouch Step – left
27. Intercept Downward in Bow Step(Right and Left)
28. Thrust Sword Down in Bow Step
29. Cloud and Slide – Right and Left
30. Chop in Right Bow Step
31. Parry and Kick backward
32. Point Sword Down in T – Step
33. Push Sword in Horse Step
34. Lift Sword over Head in One Leg Standing
35. Step Up and Stab Back
36. Burst in Low Squat with Crossed Legs
37. Thrust Back in Bow Step
38. Turn Body Around and Thrust Down
39. Raise Sword with the Tip Down and Lift the Knee
40. Thrust and Marching
41. Parry with Lotus Kick
42. Thrust Straight in Bow Step
43. Closing

彩色圖解太極武術

定價220元

定價220元

定價220元

定價220元

定價350元

定價350元

定價350元

定價350元

定價350元

定價350元

定價350元

定價350元

定價350元

定價220元

定價220元

定價220元

定價350元

定價220元

定價350元

定價350元

定價220元

定價220元

定價220元

養生保健　古今養生保健法　强身健體增加身體免疫力

定價250元

定價250元

定價250元

定價220元

定價220元

定價200元

定價160元

定價180元

定價250元

定價250元

定價250元

定價250元

定價180元

定價420元

定價300元

定價250元

定價180元

定價200元

定價360元

定價360元

定價230元

定價250元

定價230元

定價250元

定價200元

定價250元

定價200元

定價400元

定價280元

定價400元

定價300元

定價300元

定價180元

定價200元

定價200元

定價350元

定價400元

定價200元

定價280元

定價200元

定價180元

定價200元

定價280元

定價280元

定價200元

健康加油站

定價200元

定價180元

定價200元

定價200元

定價200元

定價200

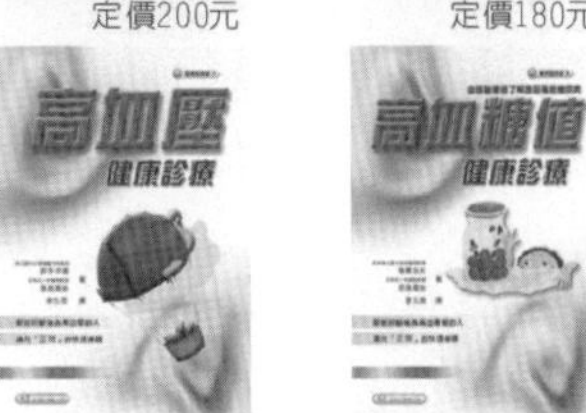

定價200元

定價200元

定價200元

定價200元

定價180元

定價180

定價180元

定價180元

定價180元

定價180元

定價180元

定價180

定價220元

定價180元

定價180元

定價200元

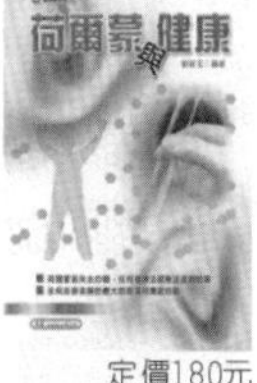

定價180元

定價200

定價180元

定價180元

定價200元

定價200元

定價200元

定價200

定價200元

定價350元

定價280元

定價230元

定價200元

定價180元

定價350元

定價180元

定價200元

定價200元

定價180元

定價300元

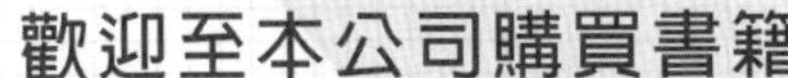

歡迎至本公司購買書籍

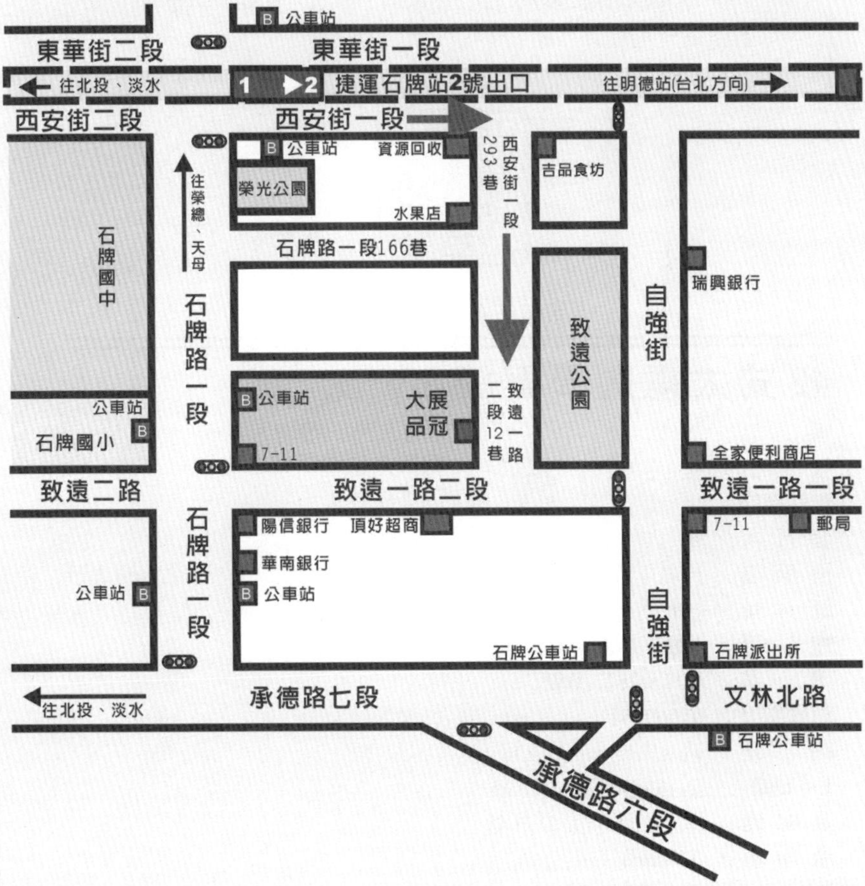

B 公車站
東華街二段
東華街一段
往北投、淡水
1 ▶2 捷運石牌站2號出口
往明德站(台北方向)
西安街二段
西安街一段
B 公車站
資源回收
293巷
西安街一段
榮光公園
水果店
吉品食坊
往榮總、天母
石牌國中
石牌路一段166巷
瑞興銀行
石牌路一段
自強街
致遠公園
B 公車站
大展品冠
致遠一路二段12巷
公車站 B
石牌國小
7-11
全家便利商店
致遠二路
致遠一路二段
致遠一路一段
陽信銀行
頂好超商
7-11
郵局
華南銀行
公車站 B
B 公車站
石牌路一段
自強街
石牌公車站
石牌派出所
往北投、淡水
承德路七段
文林北路
B 石牌公車站
承德路六段

建議路線

1.搭乘捷運．公車

淡水線石牌站下車，由石牌捷運站２號出口出站(出站後靠右邊)，沿著捷運高架往台北方向走(往明德站方向)，其街名為西安街，約走100公尺(勿超過紅綠燈)，由西安街一段293巷進來(巷口有一公車站牌，站名為自強街口)，本公司位於致遠公園對面。搭公車者請於石牌站(石牌派出所)下車，走進自強街，遇致遠路口左轉，右手邊第一條巷子即為本社位置。

2.自行開車或騎車

由承德路接石牌路，看到陽信銀行右轉，此條即為致遠一路二段，在遇到自強街(紅綠燈)前的巷子(致遠公園)左轉，即可看到本公司招牌。

國家圖書館出版品預行編目資料

42式太極劍學與練 ／ 李壽堂　編著
——初版，——臺北市，大展，2014〔民103.12〕
面；21公分 ——（中英文對照武學；5）
ISBN　978－986－346－050－3（平裝；附影音光碟）
1. 劍術
528.974　　　　103020108

42式太極劍學與練 附 VCD

編　著／李壽堂
校　訂／張連友
責任編輯／王躍平　張東黎
發行人／蔡森明
出版者／大展出版社有限公司
社　址／台北市北投區（石牌）致遠一路2段12巷1號
電　話／（02）28236031・28236033・28233123
傳　眞／（02）28272069
郵政劃撥／01669551
網　址／www.dah-jaan.com.tw
E-mail／service@dah-jaan.com.tw
登記證／局版臺業字第2171號
承印者／傳興印刷有限公司
裝　訂／承安裝訂有限公司
排版者／弘益電腦排版有限公司
授權者／山西科學技術出版社
初版1刷／2014年（民103年）12月

定價／300元

大展好書　好書大展

品嘗好書　冠群可期